Walter,

This book reminds me of our Boston Freedom trail excursion. I hope you enjoy the memories. On your next visit, we'll finish the trail.

Love,
Ann

S0-ARJ-731

Our BOSTON

Text by Jon Marcus
Photography by Susan Cole Kelly

Voyageur Press

Text copyright © 1998 by Jon Marcus
Photographs copyright © 1998 by Susan Cole Kelly

All rights reserved. No part of this work may be reproduced or used in any form by any means—graphic, electronic, or mechanical, including photocopying, recording, taping, or any information storage and retrieval system—without written permission of the publisher.

Edited by Todd R. Berger
Designed by Andrea Rud
Printed in Hong Kong

03   04   05   06   07   7   6   5   4   3

Library of Congress Cataloging-in-Publication available.
ISBN 0-89658-014-8

Published by Voyageur Press, Inc.
123 North Second Street, P.O. Box 338, Stillwater, MN 55082 U.S.A.
651-430-2210, fax 651-430-2211

Educators, fundraisers, premium and gift buyers, publicists, and marketing managers: Looking for creative products and new sales ideas? Voyageur Press books are available at special discounts when purchased in quantities, and special editions can be created to your specifications. For details contact the marketing department at 800-888-9653.

Page 1: *The Public Garden's swan boats were the idea of Englishman and local shipbuilder Robert Paget, who, in 1877, saw the Wagnerian opera* Lohengrin, *in which a knight, trying to defend his lady's honor, rides in a boat drawn by swans. Paget's family still operates the three-ton, pedal-driven swan boats, the oldest built in 1918 and the newest in 1958.*

Page 3: *Haymarket, Boston's principal open-air market, has survived highway construction, urban renewal, and the advent of the supermarket. It was originally a street market until one side of Blackstone Street was razed to make room for the Southeast Expressway in the 1950s, and the pushcarts learned to co-exist with an exit ramp. And when Faneuil Hall Marketplace was redeveloped and posh new hotels built next door, there was pressure to close or move Haymarket. But the market persists thanks to a steady stream of customers who like to haggle with the grumpy meat, fish, and produce vendors. One of Haymarket's most interesting features is embedded in the street: "garbage" cast in bronze from actual lettuce leaves, fish skeletons, and newspapers.*

Page 4: *The grand Greek Revival Custom House (at right) was completed in 1847, near the busy wharves of Boston Harbor to reflect the city's importance to the nation's maritime trade. The twenty-four granite Doric columns alone weighed forty-two tons each. The tower was completed in 1915; because it was a federal building, the Custom House could flaunt the 125-foot height restriction of the period, and became the city's first skyscraper at 495 feet. Today it is a luxury hotel.*

Page 5: *The most momentous event in U.S. history, the outbreak of the Revolutionary War on April 19, 1775, is commemorated with a Massachusetts state holiday and a parade. Counting on surprise, British troops marched confidently to Lexington and Concord on the night of April 18–19 to confiscate a cache of rebel arms, but they were preceded by riders warning of their approach. Hours later, the Redcoats were in a desperate retreat along the same route, harassed by swelling numbers of colonists, who in the opinion of the British wouldn't fight fair, sniping at the orderly ranks of soldiers from behind stone walls and trees.*

Dedication

To my favorite Bostonians: my parents.
—Jon Marcus

To Gary, my partner, with whom anything is possible.
—Susan Cole Kelly

Contents

Introduction

Boston: Living History

"Then and there the child Independence was born."
—John Adams

As certainly as the leaves change from their summer green to yellow, red, and orange, Boston's narrow streets fill every fall with rental trucks and minivans disgorging the perennial deluge of college students who account for fully half the local population. The city's scenery may seem timeless, and its collection of historic buildings probably is unmatched in America, but—with the possible exception of the traffic—little here stands still.

Boston bustles with activity. The crowded city's treasured public spaces teem from dawn to dusk with strollers, joggers, picnickers, and in-line skaters. Its sweeping river carries rowers in sleek shells and sailboats framed by arched brick bridges. Lobster boats and water shuttles chug around the harbor in the shadow of the internationally renowned aquarium, a perfect vantage point from which to watch the periodic visits of majestic tall ships to the city. The salt smell of the ocean pervades the city at high

Above: *Oliver Wendell Holmes wrote in 1858 that Boston was "the hub of the solar system," and the exact center, he decided, was the Massachusetts State House. This bronze marker is in the sidewalk at Washington and Summer Streets, a few blocks away from that building; Holmes's words were altered slightly to "Hub of the Universe."*

Facing page: *With the oldest and largest public sailing programs in the country, Community Boating offers local children the chance to sail and windsurf on the Charles all summer long for one dollar. Adults, however, pay a considerably larger membership fee. The non-profit program was begun in 1941 by Joseph Lee, a wealthy Navy veteran and school committee member, to teach city kids to sail, in spite of other boaters who turned up their noses at the arrival of the "river rats."*

tide, and the sound of gulls drowns out even the roar of traffic along the busy waterfront.

Boston is, after all, the "capital" of New England, and, as the historian Charles Francis Adams put it, New England's natural resources amount to little more than "ice and rocks and men." And so the nation's oldest major city has had to innovate and regularly reinvent itself.

It has perfected the art of adapting old structures, marrying economic revitalization to historic preservation, and in the process created a singular cityscape that blends the brick, wood, and granite of older buildings with the glass and steel of tall modern office towers. Former warehouses that date from a time when Boston dominated the world's textile and shoe industries now house trendy shops and restaurants, high-technology businesses, and the headquarters of financial investment firms that manage a quarter of all mutual fund assets in the United States. A collection of abandoned factories along the Charles River has been converted into one of the world's centers of biotechnology, and former workshops in the Charlestown Navy Yard have become state-of-the-art medical research laboratories. The traditional seafood industry, facing regulatory restrictions on fishing in New England waters, has repositioned itself as an international crossroads for importing, processing, and distribution. Giant high-tech hardware and defense firms have given way to entrepreneurial software producers. And the culinary tradition of boiled and fried seafood has been jettisoned in favor of nouvelle cuisine, from grilled sushi steak to spicy calamari in cilantro sauce.

Even Boston's oldest landmarks and historic sites evolve. Anti-British separatists used Faneuil Hall for their gatherings, of course, but it later also was the place where abolitionists condemned slavery and suffragettes denounced sexism. Today, immigrants take the oath of citizenship in the Great Hall, while the revitalized, centuries-old market on the first floor still does a brisk business. Popular debates about contemporary issues continue to rouse passions in the Old South Meeting House, staging point for the Boston Tea Party and now home to the topical Ford Hall Forum speaker series. And the African Meeting House, the oldest black church in the nation and principal platform for the abolitionists William Lloyd Garrison and Frederick Douglass, is today a center of cultural activity; hun-

dreds cram inside for regular jazz and gospel concerts.

Geographically, Boston has also changed through time. When William Blackstone arrived on the barren, windblown peninsula the Algonquin called *Shawmut*, it covered less than eight hundred acres—smaller than some modern shopping malls. Though still comparatively small, the city has increased in size considerably by annexing the formerly independent neighboring towns of Brighton, Charlestown, Dorchester, Hyde Park, Roslindale, and Roxbury—explaining why some neighborhoods within the city limits look like residential suburbs—and by filling former wetlands in the South End, South Boston, and the fashionable Back Bay, created over forty years from a fetid swamp with fill dumped from rail cars, often as frequently as once every forty-five minutes around the clock. This massive reconfiguration also helps explain why the South End wound up north of the city's center, South Boston east of the South End, East Boston north of South Boston, and the North End southwest of East Boston.

Nor are the neighborhoods particularly sedentary. The once-Jewish enclave along Roxbury's Blue Hill Avenue now is predominantly black. Dorchester has shifted from mostly Irish to primarily black and Hispanic, and Jamaica Plain from majority black and Hispanic to substantially white. By much the same evolution, the designation "South Boston Irish," once used as an epithet, is now a point of pride.

Today the neighborhoods are peopled with inhabitants who range from the descendants of Mayflower Pilgrims to new immigrants from Haiti, China, and the former Soviet republics, chess masters willing to play all comers at outdoor tables in the heart of Harvard Square, students packing the MBTA Green Line, fishermen rising at dawn, antiquers browsing near Beacon Hill, children dancing in the Boston Ballet's Christmas production of *The Nutcracker*, and New Year's revelers jamming the streets for First Night. For them, as for Oliver Wendell Holmes when he first made the famous boast in 1858, Boston is simply the center of the solar system.

First in Boston
Superlatives are commonplace in Boston.

Adjectives such as "first" and "oldest" charac-

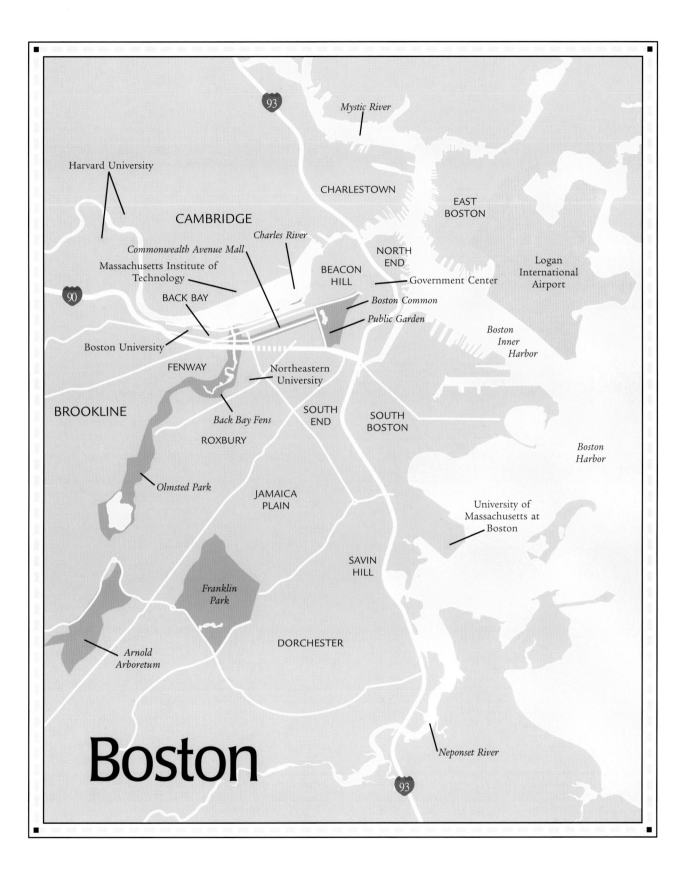

Mystic River

CHARLESTOWN

EAST
BOSTON

93

Harvard University

CAMBRIDGE

Charles River

Commonwealth Avenue Mall

Massachusetts Institute of
Technology

NORTH
END

BEACON
HILL

Government Center

Logan
International
Airport

90

BACK BAY

Boston Common

Public Garden

Boston University

Boston
Inner
Harbor

FENWAY

Northeastern
University

Back Bay Fens

SOUTH
END

SOUTH
BOSTON

BROOKLINE

Boston
Harbor

ROXBURY

Olmsted Park

JAMAICA
PLAIN

University of
Massachusetts at
Boston

SAVIN
HILL

Franklin
Park

DORCHESTER

Arnold
Arboretum

Neponset River

Boston

93

Boston has successfully married economic revitalization to historic preservation, adapting many of its oldest structures for contemporary use and thereby creating a skyline that mixes modern office towers with renovated brick-and-granite factories and warehouses. At least eight Boston businesses are two hundred years old or more, including Shreve, Crump & Low, State Street Bank, and BankBoston, the latter becoming the nation's second bank when it opened in 1784.

Why They Tahk Like That in Bawston

"It is a great pleasure to come back to a city where my accent is considered normal and where they pronounce the words the way they are spelled!"
—John F. Kennedy,
at Boston College, 1963

One of the country's most distinct regional dialects, the Boston accent has long been the source of amusement and confusion for the rest of the country, for example, over why President John F. Kennedy kept insisting there were Soviet missiles in "Cuber." Bostonians also open the "o," as in "Bawston," lengthen the "a," as in "pahk the cah," and drop the "r" as in "Hahvahd Yahd." (Beside being a source of endless ridicule, incidentally, pahking in the yahd is not allowed.)

Who's responsible? The British.

Bostonians maintained their profitable business contacts with the mother country long after the Revolutionary War, envying and emulating British culture. Among other things, they retained the British practice of dropping the "r," except between vowels, and stretching the "a," as in "auhnt."

The opposite tendency to add an "r" to words that end in vowels, such as "Cuber," linguists attribute to a phenomenon called hypercorrection. That occurs when speakers put an "r" in places they shouldn't in an unconscious bid to compensate for failing to pronounce it in places they should.

The accent "has a certain or imagined coldness to it," former Boston Mayor Kevin White, who now teaches communications at Boston University, said. "It hits the hard letters rather than the soft ones. It is not necessarily, in its first hearing, endearing."

(He actually pronounced it "hahd.")

terize not only many of the city's homes and churches, but its universities and colleges, its restaurants, its parks—even its subway system, oldest in the Western Hemisphere. Here were invented the telephone, the telegraph, the safety razor, the spark plug, the digital computer, the instant camera, medical anesthesia, the electric pacemaker, and the submarine sandwich, first served at a Scollay Square lunchstand catering to Navy sailors. The first organ transplant of any kind was conducted in a Boston hospital, and the first book and first newspaper in America were published here; the oldest Catholic newspaper still is, along with the *Atlantic Monthly,* *Banker & Tradesman,* and the *Christian Science Monitor.*

Boston also can lay claim to America's first military company, first trade union, first post office, first commercial bank, first credit union, first grand lodge of Masons, first passenger elevator, first YMCA, first football stadium, first American hockey team, first rowing club, first commercial building with electric lights, first scheduled passenger airline flight, first computer museum, and first public housing project. The city also has America's oldest restaurant, oldest continually operated tavern, oldest hotel, oldest annual marathon, oldest arboretum, oldest church pulpit in continuous use, and last manned offshore lighthouse. The world's largest annual rowing race and America's largest public sailing program call Boston home as well.

Patriots got their practice heckling Tories in the galleries of the Colonial Assembly, the first legislature anywhere that let ordinary citizens look on while it was doing business. The 1780 Massachusetts constitution is the oldest written constitution in effect in the world and was the model for the U.S. Constitution.

Of course, Boston also was the birthplace of the nation's independence, and it offers an unparalleled collection of historic settings, from the Old State House to Malcolm X's childhood home. And while it isn't covered in the tourist brochures, many of Boston's familiar landmarks were also the sites of other milestones, such as one of the world's first manned glider flights, from the steeple of the Old North (Christ) Church; and the first visit by a pope to U.S. territory, on the deck of the USS *Constitution* when the Navy flagship and the oldest commissioned warship afloat made a goodwill visit to Naples in 1849.

The city's public parks include the nation's oldest, the forty-eight-acre Boston Common—originally a communal cow pasture—from which radiate the city's narrow, angled streets; and the Public Garden, with its famous swan boats, the first public botanical garden in America.

It was in Boston that Fannie Farmer published the first modern cookbook and opened the first cooking school; later generations would learn much of what they know about food from Boston's Julia Child and Joyce Chen. The first Irish-born mayor of a major U.S. city was elected here in 1885, and the first World Series was played on the old Huntington Avenue Baseball Grounds, now the site of Northeastern University; Cy Young pitched for the Boston Pilgrims, later renamed the Red Sox. The city is headquarters to not one, but two religious sects, Christian Science and Unitarian Universalism, and to the nation's single largest producer of public television programming, WGBH, Channel 2, which originates one-third of all Public Broadcasting Service shows, including *The American Experience, Frontline, Masterpiece Theatre, Nova,* and *This Old House.*

In the nineteenth century, Boston was the unquestioned literary capital of the United States, where Ralph Waldo Emerson, Harriet Beecher Stowe, Louisa May Alcott, Henry Wadsworth Longfellow, Nathaniel Hawthorne, Henry David Thoreau, and others lived and wrote. The publishers Houghton Mifflin and Addison Wesley still are based here, and Boston continues to produce a disproportionate share of high-profile authors, including George V. Higgins, Jane Holtz Kay, Doris Kearns-Goodwin, Henry Louis Gates, Sue Miller, Robert B. Parker, James Carroll, Robin Cook, Lois Lowry,

Two lanterns were hung from the steeple of the Old North (Christ) Church as a signal that the British were coming by sea the night Paul Revere and other riders set out for Lexington and Concord to sound the alarm. But the steeple was already famous, for it was from its ninety-one-foot height that a man named John Childs flew aboard a rudimentary glider three times on September 13, 1757. Alarmed, the city fathers quickly passed a law prohibiting that sort of thing. The Old North's interior decoration benefited from some decidedly un-Christian behavior. The four cherubs flanking the organ were given to the church by a privateer who stole them on the high seas, and the sixteenth-century statue of the Virgin Mary was snatched from the prow of a luckless Portuguese vessel.

Jeremiah Healy, Cornell West, and Jane Langton.

The city is, in short, a brainy place. Almost two-thirds of the adult population have at least an undergraduate degree, and Boston leads the nation in the number of Ph.D.'s and medical doctors per capita and in the total number of Nobel laureates. The city's teaching hospitals receive about half of all National Institutes of Health research funding; of the eleven American hospitals that share the most such funding between them, nine are in Boston. There are twenty-five medical research institutions in all, more than in any other U.S. city, and thirty-three colleges and universities in Boston proper, eight in Cambridge, and nineteen more in surrounding communities, the greatest concentration in the world. As Mark Twain once remarked: In New York, they ask how much money a man has; in Philadelphia, what family he's from; in Boston, how much he knows.

It's no coincidence that intellectual Boston was home to the nation's first public school, first university, first medical school, first nursing school, first school of architecture, and first music conservatory, as well as the world's first tax-supported public library. Even the area's first white settler, William Blackstone, lugged two hundred books with him to the cabin where he lived alone on what is now the Boston Common. (Blackstone also was the first of the city's legendary curmudgeons, fleeing to Rhode Island when too many Puritans moved into the neighborhood.)

Traditional Boston

Boston's constant evolution does not necessarily make the city quick to part with its traditions. Some are as much a part of Boston's character as clam chowder or the Boston accent, and change can meet with fierce resistance.

In 1947, women staged a sit-down demonstration to prevent the old brick sidewalks of the Beacon Hill neighborhood, still lit by gas, from being replaced with cement; today, no neighborhood building or part of a building visible from the street may be altered without approval from a five-member review commission.

It took twenty-seven years of deliberation to replace the aging Boston Garden, whose rusty doors creaked shut for the last time in 1995 when Bos-

tonians finally managed to balance their nostalgia on the one hand with the dream of working restrooms and unobstructed-view seats on the other. Still, replicas of the Garden's championship banners and the original rickety parquet basketball floor were installed in the new FleetCenter as tributes to a triumphant past, while the city's knowledgeable sports fans continue to flock to historic Fenway Park.

Along with such fondness for nostalgia, Bostonians have a certain ingrained asceticism dating back to the city's origins. The austerity of its early settlers was forced upon them: Bodies were piled four deep in the cemeteries to save valuable land, for example. Later, it was an unpaid bill that sparked the deadly Boston Massacre, and the American Revolution really started in part as a dispute over a sugar tax, the Stamp Act, and a tax on tea. This frugality persists. The second-most popular destination in the city is Filene's Basement, the country's oldest and most famous discount store, where it's every-bride-for-herself at the quarterly sales of reduced-price wedding gowns.

Such Yankee thrift, combined with the success of trade and manufacturing, created Yankee wealth, and Yankee wealth produced an economic aristocracy steeped in tradition. Harvard graduates were originally lined up at commencement not alphabetically, but in order of their parents' social status. "This is good old Boston," a 1910 dinner toast went:

> "The home of the bean and the cod,
> Where the Lowells talk to the Cabots,
> And the Cabots talk only to God."

Boston also is identified with a reserve that, as with everything else here, dates to its first white settlers, the Puritans, who literally preached restraint. Well into the nineteenth century, Dickens would observe that "The peculiar province of the pulpit in New England appears to be the denouncement of all innocent and rational amusements." "Witches" and heretics—particularly Baptists and Quakers—were whipped and hanged on Boston Common, among them the Quaker Mary Dyer, who was jailed three times in conscious acts of civil disobedience before she was finally executed; and Anne Hutchinson, who was merely excommunicated and exiled but later died at the hands of Indians, a fate the Puritans smugly argued proved their point. Today, both Dyer and Hutchinson are memorialized in statues on the State House lawn.

While abstinence and anguish is more likely today to take the form of rooting for the Red Sox than self-flagellation, Puritanism of one kind or another has persisted. The city government had an official censor on the payroll from 1662 until 1975, and not until 1966 was a law banning all forms of contraception repealed. "I have just returned from Boston," Fred Allen wrote in a letter to Groucho Marx in 1953. "It is the only sane thing to do if you find yourself up there." Edgar Allen Poe professed embarrassment for having been born here. More recently, the jealously guarded independence of the residents of Boston's ethnic neighborhoods has been interpreted—mistakenly, their residents insist—as racial and religious intolerance, and was blamed for the violence of Boston's school desegregation crisis in the 1970s, an international embarrassment to a city proud of its role in the abolition movement of the nineteenth century and the civil rights struggles of the twentieth.

Despite its pious reputation, Boston's history is littered with engaging, if unseemly, indiscretions. Some of the city's solemn churches are decorated with treasures stolen on the high seas and brought to port by local privateers. Part of the family fortune that built Faneuil Hall—the "Cradle of Liberty"—came from the slave trade. Before the Revolution, Paul Revere even sold calipers to British officers to calculate artillery trajectories. The statue of John Harvard in highbrow Harvard Yard in Cambridge isn't him at all, but an undergraduate who posed for the sculptor, since Harvard left no likeness; Harvard also is misidentified in the inscription as the founder, rather than the benefactor, of the school, and the date the college was established is off by two years. The Great Dome at the Massachusetts Institute of Technology (MIT) was modeled on the Pantheon, but is more often the site of crafty pranks by students than of admiration for its architectural origins; in 1994, the city awoke to find an entire MIT police cruiser atop the dome, complete with working lights and a half-eaten box of doughnuts on the front seat, and in 1996 the whole thing was dressed up as a giant beanie.

Which is all to say that Boston generally doesn't take itself so seriously as to be a dry museum display, despite its wealth of history. Its living landmarks, bustling economy, institutions, culture and sports, parks, waterfront, and neighborhood life are chapters in a story that continues to be written: living history.

"I shall enter no encomium upon Massachusetts; she needs none. There she is. Behold her, and judge for yourselves. There is her history; the world knows it by heart. The past, at least, is secure. There is Boston and Concord and Lexington and Bunker Hill; and there they will remain forever."
—Daniel Webster, 1830

Living Landmarks

"Our family's love of history comes directly from our love
of this city and its historic surroundings."
—U.S. Senator Edward M. Kennedy

Above: *No one knows who fired first on April 19, 1775, when the British and Americans came face to face for the first time on Lexington Green. But when the smoke cleared, eight of the outnumbered colonists had been killed, and the war was on. The Americans made their stand at Concord's Old North Bridge a few hours later in a clash memorialized by Ralph Waldo Emerson as "the shot heard 'round the world"—the first real battle of the War for Independence and the beginning of the end of the international colonial system. The battles are re-enacted every year by costumed volunteers.*

Facing page: *The oldest commissioned warship afloat in the world, the USS* Constitution *was one of six powerful frigates commissioned by President George Washington in 1797 to safeguard U.S. merchant ships. She began her career bombarding Tripoli in 1805 to punish the Barbary pirates who were demanding tribute payments. But the* Constitution's *greatest victory was the defeat of the British warship HMS* Guerriere *in the first naval clash of the War of 1812 and one of the greatest sea battles of all time. She was nicknamed "Old Ironsides" by British soldiers who saw their cannonballs bounce off her sturdy oak hull. Permanently berthed at the Charlestown Navy Yard, "Old Ironsides" today has a crew of seventy active-duty officers and seamen.*

Above: *Designed by Federalist architect Charles Bulfinch to reflect the grand ambitions of the new nation, the Massachusetts State House, near the top of Beacon Hill, was acclaimed as one of the finest buildings in the country when it was completed in 1798. The distinctive dome, originally protected by whitewashed wooden shingles and later covered in copper sheathing by Paul Revere & Sons, was gilded with twenty-three-carat gold leaf in 1874, though it was painted black as a defense against air raids during World War II. The original doric columns were made of huge pine tree trunks. With the growth of government, a yellow brick extension was added at the end of the nineteenth century and two white marble-and-granite wings in 1917. Today, the building covers two city blocks.*

Right: *A Congregational church built in 1809, the Park Street Church was used to store gunpowder during the War of 1812. It is this, and not any particularly explosive oratory, that accounts for the nickname "Brimstone Corner."*

"Boston is redolent with history—in its buildings, by-ways, institutions, parks, even its subway, the first in America. It is also a good place to live—gentle in scale, walkable, at ease with its old ways and customs but alive with students, tourists and an ever-broadening population."
—Henry Lee, president,
Massachusetts Historical Society
and Friends of the Public Garden

Mary Dyer, a Quaker, was jailed three times in the 1650s for challenging Puritan anti-Quaker laws, and finally was hanged on Boston Common for sedition, one of four Quakers to be executed during the period. Her death prompted King Charles II to order the anti-Quaker measures overturned. This statue, on the State House lawn, was erected in 1959.

The most famous of Boston's graveyards, the Old Granary Burying Ground is the final resting place of Paul Revere, John Hancock, Samuel Adams, Benjamin Franklin's parents, the victims of the Boston Massacre, and seven governors of Massachusetts. Also reputedly buried here is the woman believed to be the real Mother Goose, Elizabeth Foster Goose or Vergoose, who, according to tradition, made up stories to entertain her ten children and ten stepchildren. The graveyard was named for the granary then at the site of what is now the Park Street Church. Boston's small size meant cemetery space was at a premium, but its spongy ground hastened decomposition so that, over time, many bodies could be laid to rest in tiny graveyards such as this one, where more than sixteen hundred people are believed to have been buried in the baseball-diamond-sized burial ground.

Above: *These cobblestones at State and Congress Streets mark the site of the Boston Massacre. Widely considered a zenith of the British tyranny that provoked the American Revolution, the March 5, 1770, disturbance actually was started by a young American wigmaker's apprentice who taunted a British officer, demanding payment of a debt that already had been settled. An excited colonist in the gathering mob mistook the sudden tolling of a church bell for the usual warning of a fire; when he shouted "FIRE!" the nervous British soldiers did. Five colonists were killed.*

King's Chapel was the headquarters of all colonial Anglican churches before the Revolution, but shortly afterward became the first Unitarian church in America. The pulpit is the oldest in continuous use in the United States. The first major stone building in the country, it replaced a smaller wooden chapel on the same site, which continued operating while the larger church was being built around it and was later handed out the windows, piece by piece. A planned steeple and spire were never finished, and the columns were built of wood and made to look like stone to save money. The Georgian interior was modeled on St. Martin-in-the-Fields Church in London. Elizabeth Pain, the adulteress who inspired Nathaniel Hawthorne's The Scarlet Letter, *is among the notables buried in the adjacent King's Chapel Burying Ground.*

Boston was the literary capital of America in the ninteenth century, and the Old Corner Bookstore was the literary capital of Boston. Housed there were the offices of the nation's most prestigious publishing house, Ticknor & Fields, and a bookstore where the publisher's finest authors—Ralph Waldo Emerson, Harriet Beecher Stowe, Henry Wadsworth Longfellow, and Henry David Thoreau, to name a few—passed their time. Today, Ticknor & Fields survives as an imprint of the Back Bay–based publishing company Houghton Mifflin.

Above: *The Boston Public Latin School, the first public school in America, was established in 1635; this is the site of its third home, where it opened in 1748, after meeting first in the headmaster's house and later in a building beside King's Chapel. It would move four more times before ending up on Avenue Louis Pasteur in the Fenway section, where it continues as the city's top public school and one of the nation's best. Sixth-graders take a test to be admitted to the school, which covers grades seven through twelve. Now called Boston Latin School, its alumni include Samuel Adams, John Hancock, Ralph Waldo Emerson, Leonard Bernstein, four presidents of Harvard, and four Massachusetts governors; Benjamin Franklin attended, but dropped out.*

The Old South Meeting House served as the staging point for the Boston Tea Party on December 16, 1773. After the incident, the occupying British Lighthorse Seventeenth Regiment of Dragoons retaliated by turning the Old South into a stable, using one of the pews as a pig-sty. The church was narrowly spared from the great fire that leveled much of Boston in 1872 and saved again from demoliton a few years later by Louisa May Alcott, Ralph Waldo Emerson, Mary Hemenway, and others after serving as a Civil War recruiting station and a post office. Through a popular speaker series, it still hosts fiery debates on contemporary issues.

It may look small in its veritable display case of surrounding shiny office towers, but the Old State House, rebuilt in 1748 after being gutted by fire, and the oldest public building in the city, is packed with history. In 1774, the locals locked the doors against the British and proceeded to elect a slate of delegates to the Continental Congress. The building later served as City Hall and also once housed a Masonic lodge and a restaurant before becoming one of the nation's first examples of historic preservation—though only after the city of Chicago offered to move it to Lake Michigan as a tourist attraction. Today it houses the historical collection of the Bostonian Society, including a vial of tea that supposedly fell into the boot of a Patriot named Thomas Melvill during the Boston Tea Party.

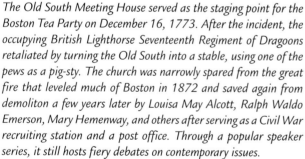

"Full of crooked little streets; but I tell you, Boston has opened and kept open more turnpikes that lead straight to free thought and free speech and free deeds than any other city of live men or dead men."
—Oliver Wendell Holmes, Jr.

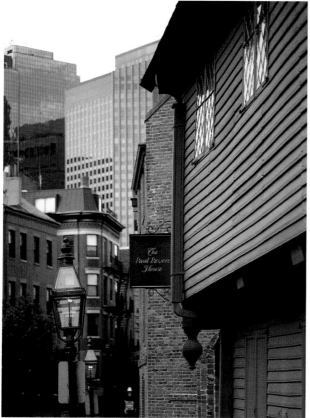

Above: *The copper-covered dome of Quincy Market. By 1824, the city had outgrown its central marketplace on the first floor of Faneuil Hall, so Mayor Josiah Quincy built this two-story Greek Revival structure next door and called it New Faneuil Hall Market; the largest development up to that time, it was later named for him. Dedicated in 1826, the 535-foot-long structure at the edge of Boston Harbor housed meat and produce stalls but fell into disrepair and eventually was abandoned. But in the 1970s, the building and two nearby structures were converted into a "festival marketplace" of restaurants, shops, and food stands. Quincy Market is still owned by the city and leased to the company that redeveloped it.*

Left: *One of Boston's oldest buildings, this house had already been around for nearly a century when Paul Revere bought it in 1770. It was from here that he slipped out of the city and set off to warn Samuel Adams and John Hancock in Lexington that British troops were marching from Boston to seize munitions hidden in the countryside. Revere was arrested on the way, and it was left to other riders to spread the alarm—despite the role imagined for him by Henry Wadsworth Longfellow in a Civil War propaganda poem eighty-five years later. Nor does the house look much like it did when Revere lived there; well-meaning preservationists lopped off the third floor, where eight of Revere's sixteen children lived. The cooking fireplace in the main room also is a mistake; the kitchen actually was in the basement.*

Above: *The final resting place of many of Boston's original settlers, Copp's Hill Burying Ground in the North End was appropriated by the British as a lookout, as a battery overlooking Charlestown, and for target training at the outset of the Revolutionary War. Among those buried there is Captain Daniel Malcolm, who contributed to the Revolutionary cause by smuggling sixty casks of wine into port without paying the duty. When he died, Malcolm was memorialized by friends in Old North Church as being "buried ten feet deep in Copp's Hill Burying Ground, safe from British bullets." In fact, his gravestone still bears the scars of British ammunition.*

Facing page: *Faneuil Hall was built by wealthy merchant Peter Faneuil in 1742, and goods have been sold on the building's lower level more or less continually ever since; the upper floors were set aside for public discourse. Called the "Cradle of Liberty," Faneuil Hall was the site of the first town meeting in America. But the discussions generally turned to the taxation policies of the British: the sugar tax in 1764, the Stamp Act in 1765, and the infamous tax on tea in 1773. Faneuil Hall became the forum for anti-slavery assemblies in the nineteenth century, temperance and women's suffrage rallies in the twentieth. Daniel Webster, Frederick Douglass, Jefferson Davis, and Susan B. Anthony all spoke here. Today the building hosts community debates, high school graduations, and naturalization ceremonies in its graceful Great Hall. On the top floor is the armory of the Ancient and Honorable Artillery Company, the nation's oldest chartered militia, which has had its headquarters in the building for 246 years.*

"Crush up a sheet of letter-paper in your hand, throw it down, stamp it flat, and that is a map of old Boston."
—Walt Whitman

"Our work takes us to the great cities of the world, but we always come home to Boston, and every time we return, we fall in love with Boston all over again."
—Patricia Harris and David Lyon, travel writers

Above: *This monument to the Battle of Bunker Hill took eighteen years to build and required the construction of the nation's first commercial railroad to carry the granite from Quincy for the 221-foot obelisk; most of the surrounding land had to be sold off to pay for it. The truth is that the colonists actually lost the famous June 17, 1775, engagement, the first major battle of the Revolution after Lexington and Concord. But it cost the British nearly half their troops, or 1,054 out of 2,200 soldiers, while the Americans suffered only 441 casualties before running out of ammunition and withdrawing. The clash actually occurred on Breed's Hill, but the British got their maps mixed up, and the battle was forever misnamed.*

Right: *Massachusetts Bay Colony Governor John Winthrop negotiated to buy the land under what is now downtown Boston from its first white settler, William Blackstone, in 1634. A Church of England clergyman, Blackstone had arrived alone on the deserted peninsula and set up house on what would become the Boston Common. In 1630, he invited his Puritan neighbors in Charlestown to join him on his side of the river, for a fee, but came to regret it when four thousand of them took him up on the offer, most seeking a reliable source of fresh drinking water. Blackstone accepted their money and moved to Rhode Island. In addition to this plaque on the Common, the city's first settler is commemorated by the Blackstone Block, the nation's oldest business block, near City Hall.*

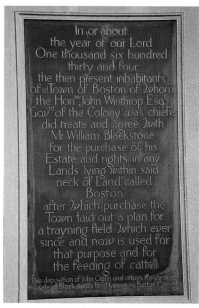

Above: *Patriots disguised as Mohawk Indians and fortified with rum protested the British tax on their second-favorite beverage with a raid on British tea ships at anchor in Boston Harbor on December 16, 1773. "Boston Harbor, a teapot tonight!" they are reputed to have shouted, sacking the holds of the ships and dumping chests of tea into the water. One of the most dramatic incidents leading to the American Revolution, the Boston Tea Party was imitated in other colonial ports and even repeated later in Boston, heightening tensions over "taxation without representation." Visitors can dump crates of "tea" from this replica of one of the original ships. However, modern-day environmental laws require that the crates be hoisted back aboard each time.*

Left: *A leader of the free black community on Beacon Hill, haberdasher John Coburn ran a gambling parlor for the upper classes in this house, which he built on Phillips Street in 1843. The wealthy Coburn became treasurer of the abolitionist New England Freedom Association and a petitioner for desegregation; he was tried and acquitted for the 1851 rescue of a fugitive slave. The house today is part of Boston's Black Heritage Trail.*

Above: *This high-relief bronze by sculptor Augustus Saint-Gaudens commemorates the Fifty-fourth Massachusetts Regiment, the all-black Civil War infantry company from Boston that was the subject of the 1990 movie* Glory. *The frieze is dominated by the likeness of its white colonel, Robert Gould Shaw, who led the July 18, 1863, assault on Fort Wagner in Confederate Charleston, South Carolina, and the monument bore only the names of the regiment's white officers when it was dedicated in 1897; the names of the sixty-two blacks who died were added in 1982. One soldier in the regiment, Sergeant William Carney, was wounded three times saving the American flag from Confederate capture, and became the first black awarded the Congressional Medal of Honor. Often decorated with bouquets by visitors, the memorial is part of Boston's Black Heritage Trail.*

Above right: *The Abiel Smith School on Beacon Hill was one of the first in the nation for the education of black children and is named for a white businessman who bequeathed money for that purpose. While Boston had the nation's first public school system, blacks were not admitted until the 1820s, and then only to substandard, segregated primary schools. The Smith School, built in 1834, took the place of makeshift schools for black children that had been run in private homes and at the African Meeting House, near this site, the oldest continuously operated black church in America. Still, some blacks boycotted the school, demanding desegregated education. The public schools were finally desegregated in 1855, and the Abiel Smith School closed. In 1887, it became the headquarters for black Civil War veterans, and it now houses the Museum of Afro-American History. The African Meeting House was dedicated in 1806; blacks had been allowed to attend white churches up until that time, but were forced to sit separately in the galleries. It later became the center of abolitionism and the place where William Lloyd Garrison founded the Anti-Slavery Society. As blacks left Beacon Hill, the African Meeting House was transformed into a synagogue in 1937, before being restored to its original appearance and reopening as a museum.*

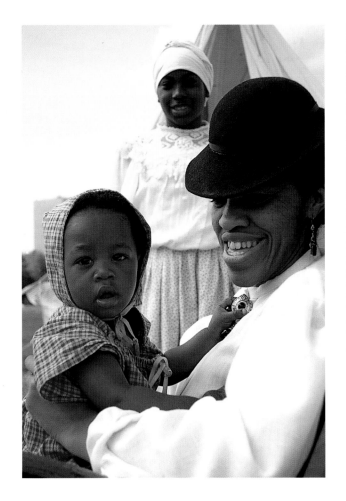

A mother and her daughters help commemorate the 100th anniversary of the Fifty-fourth Regiment Memorial. Responding to pressure from abolitionists, President Lincoln admitted black soldiers into the Union forces in 1863; the Fifty-fourth was the first recruited in the North. Despite the city's progressive reputation, many of the men were spit on as they marched to their temporary encampment on the Boston Common. The military also paid them less than their white counterparts, but the black soldiers and their white officers refused to accept their salaries for eighteen months until Congress finally relented and retroactively increased their pay.

John F. Kennedy was born on May 29, 1917, in the second-floor master bedroom of this nine-room Colonial Revival house in Brookline. His father, Joseph P. Kennedy had bought the house in 1914 and moved there with his new bride, Rose Fitzgerald. Proud of his Irish heritage, the elder Kennedy nonetheless liked rubbing shoulders with the suburban bluebloods on the trolley ride to the Financial District. All of the Kennedy children born in this house met tragic ends: Joseph Jr. and Kathleen were killed in airplane crashes and John by an assassin's bullet, while Rosemary was lobotomized. The house is now designated the John F. Kennedy National Historic Site.

"For 33 years, whether I was in London, Washington, the South Pacific or elsewhere, this has been my home. Its leaders have shaped our destiny since long before the great republic was born. Its democratic institutions have served as a beacon light for other nations. And, godwilling, wherever I serve, this shall remain my home."
—John F. Kennedy, 1961

Above: *The son of a wealthy physician, U.S. Capitol architect Charles Bulfinch was born in a comfortable mansion on this site in 1763 and attended Boston Latin School. When he was twenty-four, Bulfinch returned from a European tour inspired by architectural styles abroad. He adapted English architecture into what would come to be known as the Federalist style, a style he made prominent in Boston. He designed the State House, which was completed in 1798; oversaw the enlargement of Faneuil Hall in 1805; and designed many private homes on Beacon Hill and the West End. One of these homes, the house of mayor and later U.S. senator Harrison Gray Otis, is just a few blocks from this site; that house is now the headquarters of the Society for the Preservation of New England Antiquities and has been restored to its original appearance.*

Left: *This 115-foot pavilion, glass on two sides, is the centerpiece of the I. M. Pei–designed John F. Kennedy Library. The library houses millions of pages of Kennedy's personal, congressional, and presidential papers and the papers of his brother, Robert F. Kennedy, as well as 180,000 photographs, 5,000 audio recordings, and 8 million feet of film. The attached museum carries visitors back to the early 1960s, complete with episodes of* Leave it to Beaver *on vintage televisions in the windows of a re-created Main Street. The "Profile in Courage" Award, named for JFK's Pulitzer Prize–winning 1957 book, is conferred here each year on his birthday— May 29—by the late president's family. The award honors elected officials who show political courage by taking unpopular stands on difficult issues.*

Above: *Consistently named one of the ten greatest public buildings in the country by the American Institute of Architects, Trinity Church in Copley Square was designed by H. H. Richardson and completed in 1877. It replaced the congregation's earlier home downtown, destroyed in the great fire of 1872. Supported on forty-five hundred piles driven into the spongy landfill of the Back Bay, the church is 103 feet high at the peak of its lofty ceilings, supported atop wide columns and intricately carved black walnut beams. Its tower rises 221 feet above the square.*

Right: *The Bull & Finch Pub was famous only to the regulars who whiled away their time there until the basement tavern opposite the Public Garden was chosen as the model for the popular television series* Cheers. *The regulars have grudgingly moved on before the onslaught of fans who still come to see the place where everybody knows your name; even the cast and crew stopped by to watch the last of their 275 episodes here in 1993 after eleven years on the air. The building once was the private mansion of a wealthy family that used the basement not as a watering hole, but as a floral-arranging room*

Above: *A virtual shrine for some Bostonians and many Red Sox fans, the two-sided sixty-foot neon Citgo sign in Kenmore Square is visible for miles—most notably from inside nearby Fenway Park. The gasoline company has flashed its logo from atop this building since 1940; the current version dates from 1965 and uses 5,878 neon-filled glass tubes. A three-minute film about the lighted sign won honors at the 1968 Yale Film Festival. Once the regional offices of Cities Service Company, the building underneath the sign is today owned by Boston University.*

Left: *The New England Holocaust Memorial consists of six glass towers etched with six million numbers in memory of the Jews and others who perished in Nazi-occupied Europe. Set along a black granite path, each of the towers sits above a dark, smoldering chamber bearing the name of one of the principal Nazi death camps.*

"My first weekend at the Harvard Business School a classmate who knew Boston brought me to have dinner in a small restaurant on Beacon Hill. It was love at first sight. I said then, 'Boy, would I love to live here.' Four years later, I moved back to Boston and to Beacon Hill. That was 1964. I have lived here ever since, and have loved it."
—Thomas A. Kershaw,
owner, the Bull & Finch Pub,
inspiration for the television series "Cheers"

Life's Blood:
The Economy

"In my trip out West last year, I thought the wand of future prosperity, future empire, must soon surely be wielded by St. Louis, Chicago, beautiful Denver, perhaps San Francisco; but I see the said wand stretch'd out just as decidedly in Boston, with just as much certainty of staying."
—Walt Whitman

Above: *Boston has become a hub of large-scale construction, with massive public works, including the biggest road project in American history: the creation of an $11 billion state-of-the-art underground highway to replace the rusting elevated Central Artery. Private development in the city totals another $1 billion a year, most of it to keep up with the demand for downtown office space. Boston's hotels are the nation's busiest, with an average occupancy rate of more than 80 percent, spurring yet another building spree to add at least five thousand more rooms.*

Facing page: *The Back Bay is home to Boston's insurance and publishing industries, anchored by the John Hancock Tower. The commercial district is centered around Copley Square, whose trees, grass, and fountains enhance the distinctive buildings that surround it. Built in 1883 and redesigned in 1990, the 2.4-acre park was originally ringed by the Museum of Natural History and the early homes of the Massachusetts Institute of Technology, Harvard Medical School, and the Museum of Fine Arts. Once known as Art Square, it was later named for colonial Boston artist John Singleton Copley, America's first internationally recognized painter. Today the park is maintained by a private foundation underwritten by the neighboring businesses.*

"The Bostonian's passion for this second-hand city has turned citizen participation into the Hub's most popular sport. City dwellers agitate about architecture: they review it, protest against it, gather to save it, struggle to refine, define or simply take guided tours of it. Architecture may not be Walt Whitman's 'breakfast food,' but hereabouts it's more than frosting."
—Jane Holtz Kay, architecture critic and author, *Lost Boston* and *Asphalt Nation: How the Automobile Took Over America and How We Can Take It Back*

Above: *The thirty-three-story Federal Reserve Bank of Boston (at left), affectionately called "the washboard building," is sheathed in three million pounds of exterior aluminum. Opened on this site overlooking Fort Point Channel in 1977, the Boston Fed processes $106 billion in wire transfers each day, including $2.9 billion per day of bank checks and almost $100 million per day in cash.*

Facing page, top: *A center of the world's financial services industry, downtown Boston is the birthplace and headquarters of such major firms as Scudder, Stevens & Clark; Fidelity Investments; Putnam Investments; Tucker Anthony; Moors & Cabot; and Paine Webber. No less than a quarter of all mutual fund assets in the United States are managed here, or about $1.4 trillion in stocks, bonds, and cash—more than in any other city outside New York, Tokyo, and London. The Boston Stock Exchange lists 186 primary companies and trades twenty-two hundred securities; seven million shares change hands each day, with a market value of $60 billion. Sixteen Fortune 500 companies have their headquarters here.*

Facing page, bottom: *Most of Boston's Financial District, including this area along State Street, burned to the ground on November 9, 1872, in the costliest blaze per acre in American history. Long overshadowed by the Great Chicago Fire, which had occurred just thirteen months earlier, the Boston conflagration left fourteen people dead and sixty-five acres in ruins. The fire burned so hot that firehoses melted and ships burned at their docks. On land, 776 buildings were destroyed and insurance companies went bankrupt paying claims. Most of the business district was rebuilt within a year although officials decided it would be too expensive to straighten the skinny streets, ensuring that they would forever remain a Boston idiosyncrasy.*

"I've spent my entire career with the Copley Plaza Hotel. Over 40 years, I've seen room rates grow from $20 per night to over $300 and I've seen wonderful celebrities. I helped both Princess Grace and Elizabeth Taylor to their rooms. I'm nearly the first person guests meet when they arrive, so I'm an ambassador for Boston and the hotel. As exciting as that is, nothing gives me more pride than people, famous or not, who express fondness for Boston and the Copley Plaza."
—Frank Keenan, bellman at the Fairmont Copley Plaza Hotel

Above: *On a clear day, it's possible to see as far as Cape Cod and the White Mountains of New Hampshire from the observation deck of the John Hancock Tower, sixty stories over Copley Square. The tallest building north of New York, the tower was derisively nicknamed the plywood skyscraper after the glass popped out of many of its windows in the brisk Boston winds, requiring temporary wooden coverings until the problem could be solved.*

Right, top: *T-shirts on sale at Quincy Market. Tourism brings about 11 million visitors—900,000 of them from overseas—and $7 billion a year to Boston.*

Right, center: *A peculiarly Boston tradition, the Bridal Event at Filene's Basement offers expensive wedding gowns for a fraction of their original prices. Entire bridal parties line up around the block hours before the store opens; at least five times since the quarterly sales began in 1947, the doors have been ripped from their hinges. Fitting rooms for women weren't installed until 1991, so brides changed in the aisles—many still do, to save time. At the spring Bridal Event in 1993, the racks were cleared of twelve hundred dresses in a record fifty seconds. The country's oldest discount outlet was opened in 1908 and moved into the present building in 1912. The store is Boston's second-most-popular attraction, visited by an average of twenty thousand people daily.*

Right, bottom: *The nineteenth-century gaslit, bowfront-windowed brownstones of elegant Newbury Street house more than thirty art galleries and countless restaurants, cafes, and pricey shops. Built by the city's wealthy elite, Newbury Street also is the home of the New England Historical Genealogical Society, the oldest and largest organization of its kind.*

Facing page: *The John Hancock Tower looms above Boston's Back Bay, as seen from the Esplanade in springtime.*

"Its success in the financial services industry demonstrates that Boston is a city on the move. Today, Boston is a world-class financial powerhouse with strong representation in all aspects of the financial world and particular strength in the area of investment management. All this makes Boston a very livable and vibrant city within a geographical environment where more history exists than anyplace else in America."
—William G. Morton Jr., chairman and chief executive officer, the Boston Stock Exchange

Above: *Tourists mix with locals from the neighboring Financial District at Faneuil Hall Marketplace, the city's most popular attraction, which draws ten million people a year to its seventy shops, fourteen restaurants, forty food stalls, and comedy nightclub. Quincy Market and its two adjacent buildings have housed vendors' stalls and stores since they were completed in 1826, but the buildings were abandoned and dilapidated by the 1970s. The Rouse Company convinced the city they could be restored into a first-of-its-kind "festival marketplace," mixing shopping and dining. The enormously successful project, which opened in 1976, sparked a major downtown renaissance and inspired imitations in New York, Baltimore, and other cities.*

Right: *As famous for its surly waitresses as for its heaping family-style food, Durgin-Park was opened in 1826 by John Durgin and a silent partner, Eldredge Park; Durgin and his family had run restaurants in Boston since before the Revolutionary War. Unshaded lightbulbs still hang from the tin ceiling over long wooden tables covered by worn, red-checked tablecloths, and while the many regulars complain the tough-talking waitresses have mellowed, one thing hasn't changed: the singularly New England menu of clam chowder, lobster, Indian pudding, corn bread, broiled scrod, and venison pie.*

"There are so many people doing stimulating things [in Boston]. More than in any other place, people in the cooking industry are all friends. It's like a big family. Everyone knows everybody and helps everybody out, and it's a quite productive atmosphere."
—Julia Child

Left, top: *About forty-five thousand cars per day squeeze through the Callahan and Sumner Tunnels to East Boston and Logan International Airport. The airport is the seventeenth-busiest in the United States, twentieth-busiest in the world, with fifteen hundred takeoffs and landings daily handling twenty-five million passengers per year and 870 million pounds of freight. Built in 1934, the Sumner Tunnel was named for War of 1812 hero William H. Sumner, son of Massachusetts Governor Increase Sumner. The Callahan, shown here, was built in 1961 and named for William Callahan Jr., an infantry lieutenant in the Tenth Mountain Division killed in action just three weeks before the end of World War II. A third tunnel to the airport was opened in 1996 and named for Red Sox legend Ted Williams.*

Left, center: *More than seventy thousand people travel through South Station every day on 20 Amtrak and 207 commuter trains. The largest and costliest railroad terminal in the world when it was built in 1898, South Station was modeled on the elegant old-world rail stations. In the heyday of U.S. rail travel, it was the busiest railroad station in the country, handling more than thirty-eight million passengers in 1916—almost twice as many as Grand Central Station in New York. Saved from the wrecking ball in 1975 when it was listed on the National Register of Historic Places, South Station underwent an $80 million restoration and reopened in 1989. The station includes the only remaining hand-wound tower clock in New England, and a ten-foot granite eagle sculpted by Frédéric Auguste Bartholdi, the designer of the Statue of Liberty, is perched atop the clock tower—symbols of the speed and punctuality of train travel.*

Left, bottom: *Boston's subway system is the oldest in America, as this mural inside Park Street Station attests. By the time the subway opened in 1897, the narrow streets had become so clogged by horse-drawn trolleys that it was said pedestrians could walk to work on the roofs of the cars. The subway's first leg connected Park and Boylston Streets. Sixth-largest in the nation, the Boston subway system today carries 650,000 people per day on its four main lines, demarcated since the 1960s by the colors red, blue, green, and orange. This 110-foot ceramic sculpture stands at the site of the original excavation, and the braces visible between the panels are the original supports of the first tunnel. The mural shows vintage trolleys, tools, rail spikes, and underground ephemera.*

41

Above: *The Boston Seafood Show is the world's largest, with 750 exhibitors who catch, process, and sell live, fresh, frozen, farmed, canned, dried, and salted fish.*

Left, top: *Founded in Boston in 1901 by "King" Camp Gillette, the inventor of the safety razor, the Gillette Company today is the world leader not only in shaving products, but also in writing instruments, toothbrushes, and alkaline batteries through its Parker, Paper Mate, Braun, Oral B, and Duracell lines. This plant in South Boston is the world's largest razor blade manufacturing facility; three thousand of Gillette's forty-four thousand worldwide employees work here.*

Left, center: *A centerpiece of the Boston area's booming biotechnology industry, this $150 million Genzyme Corporation plant on the Charles River in the city's Allston section is the largest recombinant protein manufacturing operation in the world, producing the most complicated biotech drug ever made: Cerezyme, a treatment for a genetic disorder called Gaucher's Disease that causes anemia and bone erosion. The area's biotech industry has grown from scratch into more than 125 companies with $1.2 billion in annual sales; many have set up sophisticated laboratories in converted former factories along the river.*

Left, bottom: *Beer has always been an ingredient of Boston's history. The Pilgrims settled in Plymouth rather than continuing their journey at sea because "our victuals were spent, especially our beere," one later wrote, and many a Revolutionary War—era protest was plotted in a Boston tavern. The original Boston Beer Company was the oldest commercial brewery in America, founded in 1828, and one of twenty-two breweries in Boston's Jamaica Plain section by the early 1900s, most staffed by German immigrants whose impact is recalled by street names such as Beethoven, Mozart, Bismarck, and Germania. Boston once boasted more breweries per capita than any other U.S. city. Most of these small companies could not compete with larger national beer distributors, however, and eventually closed. Their revival is exemplified by the new Boston Beer Company, opened in 1984 on Germania Street. The company makes some of its Samuel Adams draft beer for the Boston market in this historic building, once the Haffenreffer Brewery. Adams himself inherited his father's malt house on State Street after graduating from Harvard in 1748, but turned out to be better at brewing rebellion than beer, and the business quickly folded.*

Above: *Four engines drive Boston's modern-day economy: financial services, health care, high technology, and higher education. Combined, those industries account for more than a quarter of all jobs in Massachusetts and support almost the same number of workers in other industries. The city benefits from its unparalleled research base; many of the fastest-growing local companies were founded by engineers and scientists working at the Boston area's academic and research institutions. The city's cultural and natural amenities persuade many of the graduates of these schools to stay, making it home to the nation's highest percentage of twenty-four- to thirty-four-year-olds with college degrees.*

Right: *One of Boston's many new microbreweries, the Tremont Brewery in Charlestown is the only one to bottle beer within the city limits. Its Tremont Ale, sold only in the Boston area, is brewed in the traditional British manner in English-made equipment using Boston city water from the Quabbin Reservoir of western Massachusetts, one of the best municipal water sources in the East for brewing. Tremont's state-of-the-art bottling line can fill and cap 110 bottles per minute. Charlestown was the location of the first brewing license in the United States, issued to Captain Robert Sedwick in 1637.*

"Boston is full of well-educated, passionate individualists. People here care about their work and want to create something wonderful and enduring. We march to our own drummers; we don't fall for the passing fads that blow through other cities like smog. That's why Boston was a great place to introduce Samuel Adams, one of the nation's first craft-brewed beers. Boston is a place where people blend centuries of history with innovation and new challenges."
—Jim Koch, founder, Boston Beer Company

Boston's Backbone: Education, Health, Government, and Religion

"I sincerely believe that the public institutions and charities of Boston
are as nearly perfect as the most considerable wisdom,
benevolence and humanity can make them."
—Charles Dickens

Above: *The "new" Old South Church was built at Boylston and Dartmouth Streets by members of the Old South Meeting House when they moved to the Back Bay. But its roots go back to the First Church near the old State House, where John Alden, son of Pilgrim settlers John and Priscilla Alden, was among the congregants. The northern Italian Gothic building was opened in 1875; its 220-foot bell tower is a 1932 replacement for the original, taller tower, which listed to one side in the spongy Back Bay landfill.*

Facing page: *Bostonians either love or loathe their City Hall; some critics deride it as the packing crate Faneuil Hall came in. Built between 1961 and 1968 after a national design competition, the Expressionist concrete structure rises from a brick base; the protruding form on the fifth floor is the mayor's office. Even those who like the building tend to dislike the surrounding plaza, which is considered too big for the city's relatively small scale.*

Right, top: *The Great Dome of the Massachusetts Institute of Technology in Cambridge, built in 1916, was modeled after the Pantheon in Rome. A favorite target for student pranks, it was secretly turned into an enormous pumpkin on Halloween in 1962 and covered with a giant red-and-white beanie in 1996. Self-described "hackers" have somehow transported a working phone booth, a life-sized fiberglass cow, and an intact dormitory room to the roof. But in perhaps their greatest feat, students managed to put a police car atop the dome in 1994, complete with flashing lights and a box of doughnuts on the front seat. Other structures on the mile-long campus along the Charles River were designed by I. M. Pei (Class of '40) and Eero Saarinen. Thirty-one MIT faculty members have won Nobel prizes, and the university's entrepreneurial graduates have founded four thousand companies with 1.1 million jobs and annual sales of $232 billion worldwide.*

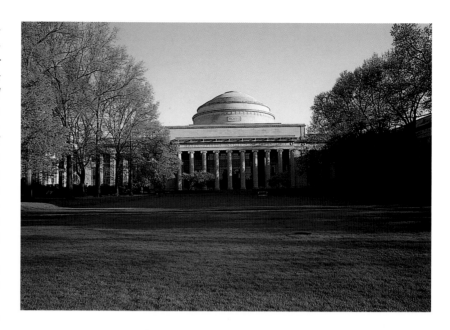

Right, center: *Harvard University's campus in Cambridge is a potpourri of architecture spanning centuries, including many Colonial-era brick structures, Federal-style buildings by Charles Bulfinch, and the lone North American commission, the Carpenter Center of the Visual Arts, of the Swiss-French modern architect Le Corbusier. Widener Library is also in Harvard Yard. It is the world's largest academic library, whose thirteen million volumes include a Shakespeare first folio and a 1520 treatise by Martin Luther. Founded only sixteen years after the arrival of the Pilgrims at Plymouth, Harvard is America's oldest university. It has grown from its original twelve students to the current eighteen thousand, with twenty-three thousand faculty and staff.*

Right, bottom: *Harvard's commencements are steeped in ceremony. Faculty members enter according to rank in ermine-trimmed velvet robes and the distinctive silk-lined hoods of the universities they attended. Graduates compete to deliver the Latin oration, and the president sits in the same wobbly chair used at every commencement since 1737. Until 1769, graduates were arranged in order of their parents' social status; now they line up in alphabetical order. Keynote speakers have used the platform of a Harvard commencement to deliver major policy pronouncements, most notably the Marshall Plan for Europe detailed in the commencement speech of General George C. Marshall on June 5, 1947. The 1884 statue of John Harvard in front of University Hall honors the young minister who bequeathed half his estate and his library of 302 books to the fledgling college.*

"We measure everything today by the
standard of Harvard"
—Professor Basil L. Gildersleeve,
Johns Hopkins University, 1886

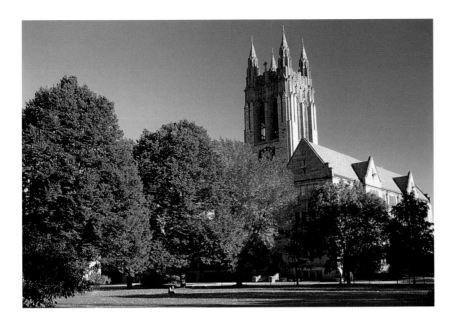

Left, top: *Founded by Jesuits in 1863 with three teachers and forty-eight students, Boston College now has an undergraduate and graduate enrollment of nearly fifteen thousand, an international reputation, and one of the best athletic programs among Boston's universities and colleges. It moved to this campus on Chestnut Hill, straddling the Boston border with neighboring Newton, in 1913. The Bapst Library is named for BC's first president, the Reverend John Bapst. Higher education pumps an estimated $10 billion a year into the area economy, employing 125,000 people.*

Left, center: *The nation's third-largest private university, Boston University has more than thirty thousand full- and part-time students, and more international students than any other U.S. university or college, on a campus that stretches for a mile along the Charles River. Founded in 1839 as the Newbury Biblical Institute in Newbury, Vermont, the school later moved to Concord, New Hampshire, before settling in Boston. It boasts the nation's oldest college of music and first school of public relations, and BU was the first university to open all of its divisions to women. It graduated the first black psychiatrist in the United States, the first woman Ph.D., and the first black woman medical doctor. The Reverend Dr. Martin Luther King Jr., F. Lee Bailey, and Faye Dunaway were graduates; Tipper Gore met her husband, Al Gore, while she was a student at BU and he attended Harvard. Among the faculty: Nobel Prize winners Elie Wiesel, Derek Walcott, and Saul Bellow, and U.S. poet laureate Robert Pinsky. Alexander Graham Bell taught at BU while he was developing the telephone.*

Left, bottom: *While Boston-area colleges and universities boast some of the nation's finest college hockey teams, few compete on the national college football stage. That doesn't stop enthusiastic crowds of students and alumni from enjoying crisp fall Saturdays under blue skies in the bleachers, in this case to cheer on the Northeastern Huskies. Spun off by the local Young Men's Christian Association, which was itself the YMCA's first American branch, Northeastern University opened as the Department of Law of the Boston YMCA in 1898 next to the site of the city's first major league baseball stadium. Northeastern has had an athletics program since 1916, one year after it was incorporated as a college, and has fielded a football team since 1933. Boston also boasts the nation's oldest football stadium in continuous use: Harvard Stadium in the Allston section.*

Brigham & Women's Hospital was created by the merger of the Peter Bent Brigham Hospital, which could claim the world's first successful kidney transplant and the invention of the iron lung; the Robert Breck Brigham Hospital, the first to specialize in arthritis and rheumatic diseases; and the Boston Hospital for Women, which conducted ground-breaking trials of oral contraceptives. The combined institution, which emerged in 1975, ranks among the nation's best.

The University of Massachusetts at Boston opened this $137 million harbor campus next to Dorchester Bay in 1974, a decade after it was founded; it merged with the former Boston State College in 1982. A commuter school, UMass Boston has an enrollment of about twelve thousand students, most of whom work to subsidize their educations. Often overshadowed by the state's renowned private universities and colleges, UMass has five campuses, the flagship in the town of Amherst and the others in Lowell, Dartmouth, and Worcester.

Consistently ranked among the nation's top four cancer research and treatment centers, the Dana-Farber Cancer Institute also is one of only thirteen federally designated centers for AIDS research. Originally called the Children's Cancer Research Center, it was founded in 1947 by Children's Hospital cancer researcher Dr. Sidney Farber, whose cause was taken up by athletes and entertainers, including Jimmy Durante and the movie mogul Louis B. Mayer. It was renamed the Dana-Farber Cancer Institute in 1983. In 1948, when the Variety Club of New England organized a radio broadcast of a visit by the Boston Braves baseball team to the bedside of a young leukemia patient named Jimmy, contributions started pouring in. The Jimmy Fund was later adopted as the official charity of the Boston Red Sox when the Braves (now the Atlanta Braves) moved to Milwaukee in 1953.

"Boston runs to brains as well as to beans
and brown bread."
—William Cowper Brann

Above: *One of the greatest discoveries in medicine occurred on October 16, 1846, in this operating theater on the top floor of Massachusetts General Hospital's Bulfinch Building when Boston dentist William T. G. Morton demonstrated the use of anesthesia, ending the terrible pain that had been associated with surgery until that time. Morton administered ether to Gilbert Abbott, a printer who had a tumor on his jaw, using a sponge and a specially designed inhaler made of glass. Abbott awoke to inform the audience of incredulous physicians and medical students that he had felt no pain. "We have conquered pain!" proclaimed a British newspaper reporting the event. Known since as the Ether Dome, this historic operating theater designed by the architect Charles Bulfinch has been carefully restored to commemorate the discovery.*

The largest and widely considered the best pediatric medical center in the United States, Children's Hospital in Boston is the primary pediatric teaching hospital of Harvard Medical School, where most of the hospital's physicians hold faculty appointments. Founded in 1869 with twenty beds, Children's Hospital now treats more than 270,000 patients annually and operates the world's largest pediatric research laboratory, named for John F. Enders, the Nobel Prize–winning scientist on its staff who was the first, in collaboration with others, to culture the polio and measles viruses.

"Boston is the place where the nation does its thinking. An unparalleled collection of colleges and universities, libraries and museums, technological institutes and medical centers makes it one of the most stimulating urban centers in the country. All this, and a rich historical heritage, too."
—Thomas H. O'Connor, historian and Boston College professor

The elegant oval chamber of the 160-member Massachusetts House of Representatives was built in 1895; the House had previously met in what is now the Senate chamber. The "sacred cod," a two-hundred-year-old carved wooden symbol of the importance of the fishing industry that hangs above the visitors' chamber, was "codnapped" by members of the Harvard Lampoon in 1933. The Massachusetts constitution, written in 1780, was the model for the U.S. Constitution and is the oldest written constitution in effect in the world.

The fifty-six-acre Government Center complex incorporates city, county, state, and federal offices across a broad brick plaza that is often used for outdoor festivals and concerts. Government Center was built on the site of Scollay Square, a rowdy neighborhood of bars, tattoo parlors, and burlesque halls frequented by sailors while in port. In an early example of urban renewal now widely believed to have been a mistake, Scollay Square and the adjoining West End were leveled in 1958, uprooting twenty-eight hundred apartments and boarding houses. The demolished buildings and houses were homes to seven thousand Irish, Italian, Greek, Polish, Albanian, Lithuanian, Russian, and Ukrainian immigrants in Boston's most varied multiethnic neighborhood. Actor Leonard Nimoy, actress Ruth Roman, and singer Buddy Clark all lived in the old West End, whose widely dispersed former residents still maintain a close network and even publish a regular newspaper.

Above: The I. M. Pei–designed headquarters of the First Church of Christ, Scientist, built between 1968 and 1975, covers fifteen acres around a 670-foot-long reflecting pool that also serves as a cooling source for the center's air conditioning system. The 1894 Mother Church is made of New Hampshire granite and has been expanded several times; today, it seats three thousand, and its organ is one of the largest in the world, with 13,595 pipes. The Christian Science Publishing Society building is home to the international daily newspaper the Christian Science Monitor. Christian Scientists believe that injuries and illness can be healed by prayer. Founded in Boston by Mary Baker Eddy, the church has twenty-two hundred branches in seventy countries.

Left: *Muhammad's Mosque No. 11 of the Nation of Islam was founded in 1954 in Roxbury by Malcolm X, who grew up in Boston in the 1940s. He pronounced himself "beside myself with joy" when the temple was established in a small room with a few folding chairs, and he served briefly as its minister.*

Cultural and Sports Diversions in the Athens of America

"In true Yankee tradition, New Englanders have patronized both the performing and visual arts in Boston. While this city is rich in history and educational institutions, it also has a diverse population experiencing the arts for the first time and returning for more. With this as a foundation, the soul of the city resounds in its love for the arts, from Broadway blockbusters to artistic ventures by not-for-profit organizations. The Boston arts community is alive and well and constantly evolving in its outreach to all."
—Josiah A. Spaulding Jr., president and chief executive officer,
The Wang Center for the Performing Arts

Above: *The Boston Marathon was the first major marathon to include a wheelchair competition, starting in 1975. Seven-time women's wheelchair champion Jean Driscoll stumbled on a trolley track in 1997, damaging her chair. She still came in second.*

Facing page: *The polished-granite Hatch Memorial Shell was the successor to a rudimentary bandstand where Arthur Fiedler conducted the Boston Pops in the first free Independence Day Esplanade concert on July 4, 1929. Named for real estate developer and auctioneer Edward A. Hatch, it was given to the city by his sister, Maria, in 1939, and designed by architect Richard Shaw. The names of some of the greatest musicians in history are etched onto the shell, which underwent a $5.2 million renovation in 1991.*

"I'd like to retire in New England. The opportunity to finish my career in Boston was what brought me back to coach the Celtics. It's refreshing to go out in the city at night, to walk down to the North End, to run along the Charles and to be made to feel welcome by everybody in the city."
—Boston Celtics Coach Rick Pitino

Right, top: *The world's oldest annual marathon, the Boston Marathon was first run in 1897, a year after a contingent from the Boston Athletic Association competed in the first modern Olympics in Athens, Greece. The athletes decided to transplant the grueling endurance contest to the Athens of America.*

Right, bottom: *From only fifteen starters in its first year, the Boston Marathon has grown to a field of ten thousand; its centennial running in 1996 attracted forty thousand. For most of its history, however, the 26.2-mile race was an informal occasion, unaffected until the 1980s by the inevitable corporate sponsorship and prize money. It was so disorganized, in fact, that someone once forgot to check the rail schedule and the route was blocked for twenty minutes by a lumbering freight train. Although the world's elite marathoners now routinely break course and world records, most of the entrants are enthusiasts who run as a hobby, not for a living. Freed from work and school by the Patriot's Day holiday, more than one million spectators line the route of the road race.*

Left, top: *Opened April 20, 1912, with a game against the New York Highlanders—later to become the hated rival Yankees—Fenway Park is one of the two oldest major league baseball stadiums; Navin Field, later to be renamed Tiger Stadium, debuted the same day. Many fans insist they come to Red Sox home games not to see the team play, but to enjoy the intimate ballpark with its 33,781 seats, manual scoreboard, short right-field line and thirty-seven-foot left-field wall dubbed the Green Monster. Three pro football teams have also called Fenway home: the Boston Redskins, now in Washington; the Boston Yanks, now the Indianapolis Colts; and the Boston—now New England—Patriots.*

Left, center: *The FleetCenter's multimillion-dollar video scoreboard is thirty feet square on each of its four sides, framing four twelve-foot video screens, and hides spotlights, laser lights, and security cameras. The scoreboard provides even more proof that the state-of-the-art building is a far cry from the Boston Garden, which was locally beloved despite its hard seats, obstructed views, and lack of air conditioning. The Garden was a place so tough, the late Grateful Dead singer Jerry Garcia once said, the rats wore leather jackets.*

Left, bottom: *Reminders of the historic dominance of Boston's two sports dynasties, these sixteen Celtics and five Bruins championship banners in the FleetCenter are replicas of the originals that hung from the rafters of the hallowed Boston Garden until it was closed in 1995. There are also banners honoring the players from both teams whose numbers have been retired. New England's largest sports complex, the $160 million FleetCenter had to be squeezed onto 3.2 acres just nine inches from the wall of the existing Boston Garden, which remained in operation during its construction; the designers compensated by making the new arena ten stories tall with very steep seating. The banners weren't the only memorabilia salvaged from the sixty-seven-year-old "Gah-den." The famous parquet floor was brought over, complete with its gaps and splinters, and the big metal letters spelling BOSTON GARDEN that graced the old facade now hang above the bar in one of the FleetCenter's three luxury restaurants.*

"Boston is quiet, but there is none of the
torpor of still life about it."
—Thomas Hamilton, *Men and Manners in America*, 1833

Right: *The Charles Playhouse has a history as entertaining as the theatrical productions that appear on its stages. Designed and built as a Universalist church in 1839, it became a synagogue in 1864, then served as a Scotch Presbyterian church and a YWCA before it was transformed into a speakeasy during Prohibition. Renamed the Rio Casino in the 1940s, the building became a fashionable nightclub with jazz downstairs featuring such artists as Fats Waller and Earl Fatha Hines. It opened as a theater in 1958 and has premiered works by Brecht, O'Neill, Pirandello, and Tennessee Williams.*

Although some plays and films were banned in Boston—the city employed an official censor from 1662 until 1975—its entertainment district thrived beginning in the early 1900s, when live musicals and plays on their way to Broadway, vaudeville shows, and motion pictures packed elegant new theaters. After a mid-century slump, the Theater District has rebounded; in 1996, five of the major theaters were again lit at the same time. Millions of dollars have been pumped into the district to renovate historic stages and bring performances to them, and audiences have returned, along with lines of cabs, long waits at the nearby restaurants, and crowds of pedestrians directed by whistle-wielding police. The Wang Center, foreground, built in 1925 and modeled after the Paris Opera Comique, underwent a nearly $10 million restoration to resume its place as the grand dame of New England theaters.

"This area is really unique in the availability and accessibility of intellectual strengths in all areas, and particularly in the sciences and also, for me, in music."
—William N. Lipscomb Jr., winner of the 1976 Nobel Prize in chemistry and classical clarinetist

Left: Built in 1910, the seventeen-hundred-seat Shubert Theatre is one of Boston's so-called "legitimate" theaters, paying union fees and wages. South Pacific, Camelot, Mame, The King and I, and Richard Burton's Hamlet are among the classics that tried out here before going on to Broadway. One of seven Boston theaters once owned by the Shubert Organization, the Shubert now is operated by the neighboring Wang Center for the Performing Arts.

The oldest and most elegant continuously operating legitimate theater in Boston, the Colonial Theatre opened December 20, 1900, with a production of Ben Hur. *George M. Cohan, W. C. Fields, Fannie Brice, Irving Berlin, the Marx Brothers, Fred Astaire, Cole Porter, Sir Lawrence Olivier, Helen Hayes, Orson Welles, Will Rogers, Danny Kaye, Barbra Streisand, Julie Harris, Katharine Hepburn, and Bob Fosse are among the greats who have performed there. Rogers and Hammerstein's* Away We Go *also premiered here; revamped and rewritten in Boston, it reopened on Broadway under its new name—*Oklahoma!

As their nervous parents wait downstairs, children ages seven to fourteen from Boston Ballet's Center for Dance Education annually audition for one of more than two hundred parts as toy soldiers, dolls, baby mice, reindeer, and angels in Boston Ballet's production of Tchaikovsky's The Nutcracker. First mounted in 1965, the Christmas-season performances attract an annual audience of 140,000 people, making this the most popular production of The Nutcracker in the world.

The Ballet Theatre of Boston also stages The Nutcracker every Christmas at the 976-seat Emerson Majestic Theatre. The twenty-member permanent company and school was founded in 1986 to make ballet accessible to all audiences with free and reduced-price tickets. It mounts new interpretations of classical ballets and is the only ballet company in New England to produce an entire repertory of original works by its own resident choreographer, in this case the Cuban-born artistic director José Mateo.

Above, left: *Made from layers of aluminum of various thicknesses, this sculpture of Arthur Fiedler near the Charles River was created in 1984 by Cambridge sculptor Ralph Helmick. Fiedler conducted the Boston Pops from 1929 until 1979.*

Above, right: *Conducted by Seiji Ozawa, the Boston Symphony Orchestra is one of the world's finest and its home, Symphony Hall, one of the world's most acoustically perfect concert venues. Béla Bartók, Leonard Bernstein, Aaron Copland, Serge Prokofiev, and Igor Stravinsky are among the composers who have written works especially for the orchestra. In 1952, the BSO became the first Western orchestra to play in the Soviet Union and, in 1979, the first to play in China. Built in 1900, Symphony Hall was designed by McKim, Mead and White, the architects behind the Boston Public Library. The hall's original oak floors, leather seatcovers, and plaster walls, carefully designed by a Harvard physics professor, help account for the superior acoustics.*

Left: *The Borromeo String Quartet, the quartet-in-residence of the New England Conservatory of Music, plays in NEC's Jordan Hall. The 1,013-seat hall was a gift of Conservatory trustee Eben D. Jordan II in 1903; it cost $120,000 to build and was restored in 1995 at a cost of $8.2 million. A national historic landmark, Jordan Hall hosts two hundred performances annually, about half of them free concerts by the Conservatory's students, faculty, and resident ensembles. Among the artists who have performed there are Emanuel Ax, Yo-Yo Ma, Stan Getz, Kurt Masur, Pablo Casals, Marian Anderson, Isaac Stern, and Benny Goodman.*

Above: *Paid for by donations and the sale of festival admission buttons, First Night was created by Boston's sizable arts and entertainment community. It includes a parade and activities such as face painting for New Year's revelers who can't stay up past their bedtime.*

Right, top: *Boston welcomes each new year with the original First Night, the oldest and largest in North America. The alcohol-free, city-wide party features more than 250 performances by about one thousand artists in forty-five venues, followed by a laser and fireworks display from the Custom House Tower and free rides home on public transportation for the estimated two million annual participants. Created in 1976, Boston's First Night has since spun off more than 160 such events in other cities around the world.*

Right, bottom: *Some of Boston's hottest nighttime destinations line Landsdowne Street behind Fenway Park, including piano bars, billiard halls, and the nightclubs Avalon, Axis, and Mama Kin, the latter owned by members of the Boston-based rock band Aerosmith. Thanks in part to its wealth of students, Boston is a contemporary music mecca. Among the vocalists and groups that launched their careers there: Boston, the Cars, the Mighty Mighty Bosstones, Letters to Cleo, Tracy Bonham, and Morphine. Other of the city's top clubs are clustered in Allston and downtown near the theater district.*

Above: *Widely considered one of the world's finest, the Museum of Fine Arts has more than a million objects, including Egyptian mummies, Paul Revere silver, Gilbert Stuart's unfinished portrait of George Washington that was used as the model for the one-dollar bill, and a huge Impressionist collection, including thirty-eight works by Claude Monet—the most outside of France. The MFA's first exhibitions were displayed in the Boston Athenaeum in 1876, and the collection found a more permanent home at Copley Square that same year; the Huntington Avenue building opened in 1909. The murals around this staircase were painted by John Singer Sargent and are based on stories from Greek mythology; Ziegfeld Follies chorus girls, then appearing at the Colonial Theatre, served as models for the demigoddesses.*

"Few cities have an array of world famous cultural, medical and academic institutions like Boston's. The scale and character of our neighborhoods—filled with more than 350 years of history, people, stories and events—give this city its uniqueness. You can relax overlooking the harbor or in one of many serene, tranquil open spaces, all while still only minutes from our thriving downtown."
—Mayor Thomas M. Menino

Left: *Multimillionaire philanthropist Isabella Stewart Gardner intended this 1901 mansion in the Fenway section, now the Gardner Museum, to resemble a fifteenth-century Venetian palazzo, even importing whole stone arches and columns from Europe. The first three floors were filled with Gardner's extraordinary art collection and were open to the public; she lived on the fourth floor until her death in 1924. The courtyard is filled with plants and trees beneath a glass roof that lets in natural light. The only museum in which a single person both assembled the art and oversaw the construction of the building, the Gardner exhibits twenty-five hundred objects spanning thirty centuries and is particularly rich in Italian Renaissance pieces. In one of the biggest art thefts in history, two burglars dressed as Boston police officers stole thirteen works of art valued at $300 million from the Gardner in 1990, including works by Rembrandt, Vermeer, and Degas.*

Above: *Originally designed as a research tool to study the structure of atoms, the world's largest Van de Graaff generator now lets visitors to Boston's Museum of Science witness a lightning storm at close range. The air-insulated generator, created by Robert Van de Graaff, was given to the museum by the Massachusetts Institute of Technology. Thirty-seven feet tall, it can produce up to 2.5 million volts of electricity and sparks fifteen feet long. The generator is housed in the Thomson Theater of Electricity, named for Massachusetts native Elihu Thomson, who invented the electric meter and co-founded General Electric. Established in 1830 as the Boston Society of Natural History and renamed the Museum of Science in 1949, the museum was the first to encompass all the sciences under one roof.*

Above, top: *Established by a group of teachers in Jamaica Plain in 1913, the internationally recognized Children's Museum pioneered the use of interactive exhibits. It moved to its current location on the Boston waterfront in 1979.*

Above, bottom: *Boston's Computer Museum, the world's first, is built around a one-of-a-kind working model of a personal computer the size of a two-story house, with canyons of printed circuit boards loaded with suitcase-sized chips. Children and adults can also try out virtual reality, pilot a DC-10, and meet the original R2-D2 from the* Star Wars *movies.*

"The proper Bostonian is not by nature a traveler. The Beacon Hill lady who, chided for her lack of travel, asked simply, 'Why should I travel when I'm already here?' would seem to have put the matter in a nutshell."
—Cleveland Amory, "The Proper Bostonians"

Above: *The Boston Public Library was the first publicly supported library in the world, founded in 1848. The present building was designed by Charles Follen McKim in 1887. The main library building in Copley Square is considered one of the foremost examples of nineteenth-century American architecture and is decorated with paintings by John Singleton Copley and John Singer Sargent and sculptures by Augustus Saint-Gaudens and Daniel Chester French, whose works include the Lincoln Memorial. This marble staircase leads from the majestic lobby to the cavernous Bates Hall reading room under newly restored works by the French muralist Pierre Puvis de Chavannes in his last major commission. The library was the first to allow patrons to borrow books, first to institute a system of branch libraries, and first to have a children's room. It remains the largest public research library in New England and the only public library that also serves as a presidential library, housing the personal papers of President John Adams.*

Left: *Founded in 1807, the Boston Athenaeum is one of eighteen remaining membership libraries in the United States. It has 5,000 members, including 1,049 proprietors who own one share each, which, until 1970, were traded on the Boston Stock Exchange. The Athenaeum was the center of the city's intellectual and cultural life in the nineteenth century; its holdings include George Washington's personal library, the largest collection of documents published in the South during the Civil War, and a collection of art so extraordinary that it was the basis for the Museum of Fine Arts. Past members have included John Quincy Adams, Ralph Waldo Emerson, Henry Wadsworth Longfellow, and Daniel Webster. The current building dates to 1847 and is a national historic landmark.*

"A sense of history pervades the neighborhoods in which we live and the cultural institutions which define Boston, from the Red Sox to the Pops. But there's also something young here—a restlessness and newness that is fostered, at least in part, by all the institutions of learning that call Boston home. The heat generated by this old-versus-new friction comes in the form of creative energy. As a performing artist, I can't imagine a better place to live and work."
—Keith Lockhart, conductor,
the Boston Pops

Living Spaces:
Boston's Parks
and Ponds

"Other cities have taken away the livability by destroying their beautiful old buildings or their parks. I spend a fair amount of time outdoors, and I love the beauty of nature, and I think we've kept that here."
—Bill Rodgers, four-time Boston Marathon champion

Above: *Hassidic Jews light a Hanukah menorah on Boston Common. The nation's oldest park, the forty-eight-acre, five-sided Common was created in 1634 as a communal cow pasture; the cows were banished in 1830. It was here that "witches" and heretics were hung, the occupying British camped, and the colonial militia mustered for the Revolution. Civil War soldiers were recruited and drilled, anti-slavery meetings held, and World War II victory gardens planted on this site. More than 100,000 people greeted Charles Lindbergh here after his historic flight, and an even larger crowd attended an outdoor papal mass in 1979 when Pope John Paul II visited the city. During the holiday season, fifty-four trees are strung with colored lights.*

Facing page: *Considered one of the finest equestrian statues in America, this immense bronze sculpture of George Washington faces the Arlington Street entrance to the Public Garden. Sculptor Thomas Ball spent months in local stables studying the horses. His only lapse: This horse has no tongue. Washington's sword has been broken so many times since the statue was erected in 1869 that the current saber is made of easily replaceable fiberglass. The flowers in the Public Garden are changed according to the season. In the spring, brilliant red and yellow tulips are planted.*

"Boston has its history, of course, but also parks and gardens, theaters, the river, beaches and perhaps the finest colleges and medical facilities in the world. It's a super sports town with a thriving and energetic business community and the best seafood anywhere —all in an area much smaller than the average city, easy to walk around in and with a feeling somehow of security and safety."
—Ethan Allen V

Above: *This once-swampy section of the Boston Common was a mudhole used to water cows until it was converted into genteel Frog Pond in 1848, as part of celebrations to commemorate the opening of the municipal water supply to replace brackish wells and cisterns. It now serves as a public wading pool in summer and as a skating rink in winter. The Common is the anchor of landscape architect Frederick Law Olmsted's nine-mile "Emerald Necklace" of nine interconnecting parks and parkways, the oldest park system in the country. The city has 3,180 acres of public and private open space, or about 6 acres for every one thousand people.*

The first and possibly the finest public garden in the United States, the twenty-four-acre Public Garden has fifty-seven flower beds filled with colorful pansies, tulips, roses, and begonias. Seven hundred fifty trees and shrubs and twenty weeping willows surround the garden's three-acre artificial lagoon. Populated by ducks and swans, the lagoon is spanned by what was originally the world's smallest suspension bridge, although the bridge has been reinforced with girders and its suspension cables are now merely decorative. The garden was begun by private donors in 1837.

Left: *Part of Olmsted's Emerald Necklace, the Commonwealth Avenue Mall became the center of the elegant new Back Bay neighborhood, which was created by filling in the original marshlands beginning in the 1850s. The one-hundred-foot-wide mall, thirty-two acres in all, was designed in 1856 in the style of a French boulevard. Olmsted called it "the finest street in the city." This statue, one of seven on the mall, depicts Revolutionary War hero General John Glover, leader of the regiment of Gloucester fishermen who ferried Washington and his army across the Delaware. Having spent his fortune to aid the American cause, the general worked after the war as a shoemaker.*

The James P. Kelleher Rose Garden in the Back Bay Fens has more than one hundred varieties of roses among two thousand rose bushes. It is the largest rose garden in Boston and one of two along the Emerald Necklace; the other is in the Franklin Park Zoo. The Fens itself, named for the saltwater marshes of eastern England, was built in 1879 and transformed a disease-ridden tidal basin that smelled of sewage at low tide into a wooded park of gentle hills. It also is the site of the Richard Parker Victory Gardens, the oldest surviving wartime victory garden in the United States; vegetables and flowers have been planted in and harvested from the four hundred plots since 1941. Boston has 117 community gardens.

Above: *The Riverway is a mile-long park built in 1881 to continue the sanitation project begun in the adjoining Back Bay Fens. This landscape is entirely man-made; even the Muddy River was rerouted to conform to Olmsted's plan. The river shares the space with a parkway for cars, paths for pedestrians, bicyclists, and horseback riders, and the MBTA's Riverside trolley tracks, all in a space only forty-five yards wide at its narrowest point.*

Right: *Frederick Law Olmsted left his mark on much of Boston's landscape; ironically, he changed the least the park that bears his name. Olmsted Park along the Riverway includes Leverett Pond at its northern border and Ward's Pond at its southern, both popular bird-watching sites; a red-tailed hawk is pictured here. The Park's original steep banks, wooded hills, groves, and meadow remain virtually untouched, although in modern times a neighborhood baseball diamond has been added.*

Above: *Scarborough Pond, a man-made seven-acre lake inside Franklin Park, was named for one of Boston's original seventeenth-century settlers, John Scarborough, who owned much of the land on which the park was later built. The biggest link in landscape architect Frederick Law Olmsted's Emerald Necklace of parks, the 520-acre Franklin Park has been rescued from mid-century neglect, and its busy public golf course, second-oldest in the United States, has been restored. Crossed by two granite bridges, Scarborough Pond is a popular spot for picnicking, fishing, and hiking.*

Left: *Jamaica Pond is a natural kettle hole, or ancient glacial pond, sixty-two acres in area and fifty-three feet deep. With its natural spring, it was an early reservoir for downtown Boston's water supply and a popular summer destination for the city's wealthy. During the nineteenth century, the pond was used to make ice until the city bought it in 1890 to create a public park that remains the center of the Jamaica Plain section of the city. A second, smaller kettle hole, now dry, is used as an amphitheater for summer stage productions. Bicyclists, runners, and walkers use the paths around Jamaica Pond, and rowboats and canoes, originally furnished as much to enhance the idyllic scene as for their recreational value, still can be rented during July and August.*

Above, left: *The 265-acre Arnold Arboretum in Jamaica Plain is the nation's oldest. It is part of the Emerald Necklace of parks designed in the late nineteenth century by land-scape architect Frederick Law Olmsted. Founded in 1872, it is today an international center for botanical research operated by Harvard University, with 15,000 living plants and 4.8 million dried specimens. Arnold Arboretum is also a beautiful spot to kindle a romance.*

Above, right: *The Franklin Park Zoo is drawing a new generation of visitors to its $26 million domed African Tropical Forest, which features four western lowland gorillas as well as leopards, hippos, tapir, warthogs, monkeys, saddle-billed storks, and hundreds of free-flying birds.*

Right: *America's first garden cemetery and an inspiration for its public parks, Mount Auburn Cemetery in Cambridge was meant as much for the living as for the dead. Founded in 1831 by the Massachusetts Horticultural Society, Mount Auburn is a vast outdoor museum of monuments, statues, and landscaping, including carefully tended rare plants and trees. More than eighty-nine thousand people are buried there, including some of America's most famous figures: Charles Bulfinch, Dorothea Dix, Mary Baker Eddy, Fannie Farmer, Felix Frankfurter, R. Buckminster Fuller, Isabella Stewart Gardner, Oliver Wendell Holmes, Winslow Homer, Julia Ward Howe, Henry Wadsworth Longfellow, Bernard Malamud, Colonel Robert Gould Shaw, and B. F. Skinner.*

"One hundred years ago, the creation of the Emerald Necklace showed how a link of nine parks could form a greenway to serve as a refuge from the hustle and bustle of the city. One can retreat to the 'wilderness' of a woodland at Franklin Park, explore the 265-acre treee museum that is the Arnold Arboretum, fish for salmon or trout in the 50-foot-deep kettlehole of Jamaica Pond, enjoy the peaceful beauty of the Public Garden from a Swan Boat and ice-skate on an outdoor rink on the oldest park in the country, the Boston Common."
—Pamela Snow, Boston park ranger

Left: *Frederick Law Olmsted moved his home and office to this sprawling property in suburban Brookline in 1883 and named it Fairstead. Considered the father of American landscape architecture, Olmsted supervised the construction of New York's Central Park, designed Boston's five-mile Emerald Necklace and the U.S. Capitol grounds, and advocated the preservation of the Yosemite Valley and Niagara Falls. He considered public parks the bastions of the democratic ideals of community and equality. At Fairstead, Olmsted, his sons, and their associates worked on five thousand landscape projects in forty-five U.S. states and in Canada. The estate is now administered by the National Park Service.*

"I love driving a cab in Boston. This is my city. It's my pride and joy. It's clean. It's safe. It's small enough that it's quaint and it's big enough that you can find everything you need. It's walkable. It's manageable. What's not to like?"
—Crystal Koufopoulos, taxi driver

The heart of the Financial District, Post Office Square replaced an ugly municipal parking garage in 1992 with an enormously popular 1.7-acre public park where office workers spend their lunch hours lounging on the sunny lawn and listening to free live music. The $80 million park was underwritten not by the city, but by the businesses surrounding it, among them Boston's richest and most powerful, and by shareholders who were guaranteed the right to lease a parking space inside the seven-level garage beneath it—the deepest excavation in the city. Proceeds from the garage, which includes an underground marble twenty-four-hour lobby with telephones and rest rooms, go to maintain neighborhood parks around the city. The post office after which the square is named was the first in the thirteen original colonies.

A 174-acre urban sanctuary, Mount Auburn Cemetery is the home to various species of wildlife, including these painted turtles that live along one of its four ponds. Spotted salamanders, rabbits, and other animals also live inside the cemetery, along with flocks of birds including yellow-bellied sapsuckers, wrens, robins, kinglets, thirty-five species of warblers, sparrows, sandpipers, hummingbirds, cuckoos, nighthawks, waxwings, orioles, and herons.

Above: *The seventy-foot Soldiers and Sailors Monument tops Flag-staff Hill on Boston Common. The four granite figures near the top of this highly symbolic monument represent the sailor, the soldier, the muse of history, and peace. The figures at the bottom stand for the eastern, northern, southern, and western sections of the country. And the bronze, bas-relief faces show the departure of Civil War troops for battle, the assault on Fort Sumter, the return of the soldiers from war, and, for some reason, the achievements of the Boston Sanitary Commission. Even the poet Henry Wadsworth Longfellow is depicted. A statue, supposedly representing the genius of America, sits at the apex of the central granite column.*

Right: *Runners, bicyclists, in-line skaters, strollers, picnickers, and sunbathers share the Esplanade, the greenspace along the Boston side of the Charles River. Formally named the Storrow Memorial Embankment, the park was built in 1931 with a $1 million gift from philanthropist Helen Storrow on the condition that plans to build a road beside it be abandoned. After Storrow died, the road was built anyway in one of the biggest construction controversies in the city's history. In a final indignity, officials named it Storrow Memorial Drive.*

America's
Front Yard:
The Waterfront

"Seeing the skyline of Boston at sunset as I'm sailing in after a day of whale
watching is one of the most beautiful sights I know—that and the sight
of a 35-ton humpback whale breaching."
—Ken Wright, whale watch captain, New England Aquarium

Above: *The USS* Constitution *takes to sea under tow each July 4. Freshly swabbed and polished after
three and a half years in dry dock, "Old Ironsides" marked her bicentennial in 1997 by triumphantly
sailing under her own power for the first time in 116 years. Since no one alive remembered how to sail the
three-masted, square-rigged warship, her twenty-seven miles of rigging had to be re-created from 1920s
photographs, and naval historians dug up the 1819 "Young Sea Officer's Sheet," instructions given cap-
tains in the British Royal Navy.*

Facing page: *A full-scale, working replica of the Boston Tea Party ship, the HMS* Beaver II, *is anchored
just yards away from the original mooring at Griffin Wharf, which has since been filled in to expand the
waterfront. On December 16, 1773, rebels marched on Griffin Wharf from an angry rally at the Old
South Meeting House to dump tea from several anchored British ships, as a protest against an unpopular
new tax imposed by Parliament. The event is re-enacted by costumed Patriots every year, on the Sunday
nearest to the anniversary. Admission charges to the ship and museum are suspended that day and com-
plimentary, tax-free tea is served.*

Left, top: *Lobster boats have returned to the once-polluted Boston Harbor. About ten million pounds of seafood is landed annually in the port of Boston, part of an industry that employs nearly twenty-five thousand people and pumps more than $7 billion a year into the regional economy.*

Left, center: *Tugboats docked in East Boston. Maritime cargo is loaded and unloaded in South Boston, East Boston, and Charlestown. The biggest exports are fish, wood, paper products, pharmaceuticals, toiletries, disk drives, integrated circuits and other electronics, textiles, and marine parts. Among the fastest-growing markets for New England trade are such nontraditional partners as Kuwait, Finland, Indonesia, and Honduras.*

Left, bottom: *Lavish pleasure boats, weather-beaten commercial boats, and even tiny houseboats tie up at the Constitution Wharf, with the Financial District in the background. Many of the surrounding wharves have been converted into restaurants, hotels, offices, and condominiums.*

Top: *Boston's Financial District viewed across the harbor at sunrise.*

Above, left: *Drawn by the dramatic views along the Atlantic seaboard—especially during fall foliage season—oceangoing cruise ships call at Boston's Black Falcon Cruise Terminal more than sixty times a year. That's up dramatically from the thirteen ship visits in 1985, and from 11,700 passengers per year then to more than 107,000 now. The booming business brings an estimated $30 million annually to the economy. Other boats based at Rowe's Wharf and Long Wharf nearer the Financial District offer whale-watching excursions, scenic tours, and dinner cruises.*

Above, right: *The harborside World Trade Center hosts twelve hundred events per year, the most of any convention center in North America. The complex was built in 1986 by converting three huge 1901 warehouses. Function rooms for weddings and meetings, with extraordinary skyline views, were added as part of the $100 million renovation, underwritten by Fidelity Investments. The flags of thirty-eight nations fly from flagpoles circling the building.*

Above: *Fort Independence on Castle Island in South Boston was dedicated in 1799 by President John Adams, but there had been fortifications of some sort or another on the site since 1634. George Washington captured the fort from the British during the Revolutionary War to end the siege of Boston. The story of a young army officer entombed alive in the dungeon was the basis for "The Cask of Amontillado" by Edgar Allan Poe, who was stationed at Fort Independence as an army private. Though closed as a fort in 1879, Fort Independence served as a military command post through World War II. Castle Island is now a popular park; volunteers from the Castle Island Association give guided tours in period uniforms.*

Left, top: *The $3.7 billion Boston Harbor Project has dramatically cleaned up Boston's famously polluted harbor. This sewage treatment plant on Deer Island can handle 1.2 billion gallons of waste per day from forty-three Boston-area communities. The waste is treated through a chemical process in sixteen of these fourteen-story, egg-shaped tanks; the process produces fertilizer and reusable methane, hydrogen, ammonia, and sulfur. Three hundred and fifty years of neglect left Boston Harbor one of the nation's dirtiest. Now dolphins, loons, and harbor seals have returned, and the city has reopened harbor beaches for swimming.*

Left, center: *The nation's first lighthouse, built on Boston Harbor's Little Brewster Island in 1716, the ninety-eight-foot Boston Light is the only remaining manned offshore lighthouse in America. Boston's thirty-four harbor islands have served as homes to forts, burial grounds, hospitals, poorhouses, prisons, and quarantine sites. In 1996, the Boston Harbor Islands became a National Recreation Area.*

Left, bottom: *One of America's most elaborate forts, Fort Warren on George's Island took twenty-four years to build with huge granite stones brought on special boats from Quincy's quarries; when the first Union soldiers arrived for training in 1861, it still wasn't finished. Fort Warren was eventually converted to a prison for twelve hundred Confederate soldiers and sympathizers, including Alexander Hamilton Stephens, vice president of the Confederacy. It is said to be haunted by the Lady in Black, a prisoner's wife sentenced to death as a spy and hanged in a black robe made from the drapes in the mess hall.*

The opening of the New England Aquarium in 1969 helped spark a rejuvenation of the Boston waterfront. The building wraps around a 200,000-gallon ocean tank, one of the largest in the world, and is home to 17,300 living fish, birds and animals—including 48 penguins.

The Harborlights Pavilion on Fan Pier seats forty-eight hundred for summertime concerts under a billowing white tent with a spectacular sunset view of the skyline.

The city's top restaurants annually ladle out an estimated two thousand gallons of New England clam chowder in the competition for the coveted title of "Boston's Best Chowder." Thousands sample the seafood soup and cast their votes during Harborfest, a six-day festival begun in 1982 to celebrate Independence Day, Boston's role in the American Revolution, and the city's maritime heritage. About two million people attend the 160 Harborfest events, which include walking tours, historical reenactments, visits from U.S. and foreign naval ships, fireworks, and concerts.

Above: *The Boston area has been a world center of rowing throughout much of its history. Irish immigrants raced professionally here in front of wagering spectators in the mid-nineteenth century, when rowing was the nation's biggest organized sport. When these contests abruptly ended under allegations of fraud, they were replaced by collegiate competitions. The first U.S. intercollegiate athletic event of any kind was a rowing race between Harvard and Yale in 1852. Elite private colleges and a few public universities and military academies have continued to dominate rowing events since then, though a Roxbury housing project in 1994 produced the first all-minority crew to enter the Head of the Charles Regatta.*

Right, top: *The world's largest rowing event, the two-day Head of the Charles Regatta annually draws 250,000 spectators and 5,600 rowers from around the world compete in nineteen divisions. The winning shell in each division takes home the honorary title "Head of the Charles." Established in 1965 by members of the Cambridge Boat Club and an English rowing coach from Harvard, it was modeled on the British "head" race, a traditional three-mile regatta in which boats starting fifteen seconds apart race against each other and the clock.*

Right, bottom: *A summer sunset plays its light against the skyline and the Charles River.*

Facing page: *Autumn on the Esplanade with the Back Bay as a backdrop.*

Bostonians All:
The Neighborhoods

"I was born down on A Street,
Raised up on B Street;
Southie is my hometown.
There's something about it,
Permit me to shout it;

We're the tops for miles around.
We have doctors and scrappers, preachers and flappers,
Men from old County Down;
Say they'll take you and break you,
But they'll never forsake you,
In Southie, my home town!"
—**South Boston song**

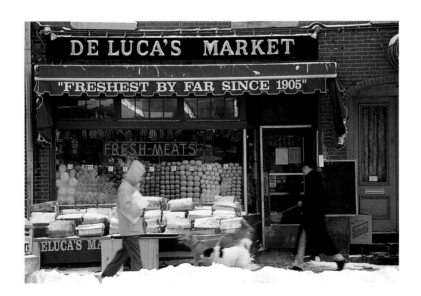

Above: *Founded as a wine and cheese shop in 1905 by Joey De Luca, De Luca's Market on Charles Street is a Beacon Hill institution. When De Luca later added a grocery store, the wine shop was moved downstairs. Its modest facade notwithstanding, De Luca's is the supermarket to the stars. Celebrities, senators, and sultans who live in or visit the exclusive neighborhood have house accounts there, but so do students and starving artists.*

Facing page: *Italian immigration to the North End began in the 1890s, and by 1920 the neighborhood, which had been the home of large Irish Catholic and Jewish populations, was 90 percent Italian and overwhelmingly Roman Catholic. Huge crowds fill the narrow streets in the summer for feasts and processions like this one, honoring the favorite Catholic saints.*

Above: *Bostonians on the Commonwealth Avenue Mall.*

Right: *Cobblestoned Acorn Street is probably the most photographed roadway on Beacon Hill, ironic since the houses along the steep, narrow passage were originally the simple quarters of the servants, coachmen, and tradesmen who catered to the neighborhood's elite.*

"To me, Boston is a city of architectural delight. The eighteenth-century legacy of twisting paths creates surprises at every turn, as historic treasures nestle side by side with a modern city. But its real magic is the seductive pallet of brick and granite, cobblestone and clapboard, waterfront and commons, woven into an intimate scale that makes it a truly livable city."
—Peter Kuttner, president, Boston Society of Architects

"I love Boston's schizophrenia. On the one hand, it's a city of fiercely proud ethnic enclaves ruled by feudal—and often feuding—warlords who jealously guard their turf, nurse every grudge and seek revenge, all while ruthlessly refusing to assimilate. On the other, in academia, medicine, finance and the cyberworld, Boston's a sophisticated player on the international stage."
—Craig Unger, editor, *Boston Magazine*

Above, left: *Saucer magnolias in the gardens of the Back Bay as spring returns in April.*

Above, right: *Boston's most exclusive neighborhood, Louisburg Square on Beacon Hill is still illuminated by gaslight, and the tiny oval park in its center is maintained with annual dues paid by the owners of the multimillion-dollar Greek Revival houses. The literati who have lived here range from Louisa May Alcott and William Dean Howells in the nineteenth century to novelist Robin Cook and Pulitzer Prize–winning playwright Archibald MacLeish in the twentieth.*

Left: Make Way for Ducklings, *the classic children's book by Maine author Robert McCloskey about a family of ducks that lives in Boston's Public Garden, comes to life each Mother's Day during the Make Way for Ducklings Parade for children and their parents. Mrs. Mallard, matriarch of the famous fictional family of fowl, and her ducklings—Jack, Kack, Lack, Mack, Nack, Ouack, Pack, and Quack—were memorialized in life-sized bronze in 1987 in the Public Garden. In 1990, First Lady Barbara Bush was so taken with them she arranged for an identical sculpture to be sent to Novodevichy Park in Moscow as a gesture of friendship.*

Above: *From its intolerant Puritan origins, greater Boston has come to be the home of exotic international cultures. Held in February in Cambridge, the Losar festival celebrates the Tibetan new year. About 180 Tibetans call Cambridge home.*

Right, top: *Fixtures of cerebral Harvard Square, sidewalk chessmasters take on challengers in front of knowledgeable audiences. Many of the quiet shops that once defined the square have been replaced by stores more common to suburban shopping malls, as landlords cash in on the cachet by raising rents beyond what many smaller businesses can pay. And yet the archetypal college town remains a place where students mix with aging hippies, classical musicians play for quarters, and scholars linger, reading books at tables in front of sidewalk cafes and ignoring the advance of chains that sell designer clothing, gourmet cookies, natural cosmetics, and CDs.*

Right, bottom: *The Cantab Lounge in Central Square in Cambridge opens its stage to poets every Wednesday night at "Da Slam," the area's most popular poetry slam. Young, literate, and multiethnic—yet not so hip that rental and restaurant prices have become exorbitant—Central Square is a favorite hangout for students from all over the Boston area.*

"What I love best about Boston is that the heritage of great American craftsmanship can be seen in the centuries-old brownstones and townhouses that line the city's neighborhoods. My hope is that, as stewards of the city, future generations of Bostonians will continue this tradition."
—Norm Abram, master carpenter,
"This Old House" and "The New Yankee Workshop"

Burned to the ground by the British after the Battle of Bunker Hill in 1775, independent Charlestown was rebuilt following the Revolutionary War. It developed into an affluent community that included the Charlestown Navy Yard and several industrial companies, including the Schrafft Candy Company and the Diamond Match Company. Charlestown retains the elliptical street pattern laid out by the Puritans who settled there in 1628. Long connected to Boston by ferry, Charlestown was annexed in 1874. Today it is home to a mix of blue-collar natives and recently arrived white-collar professionals attracted by the skyline views, close proximity to downtown, and charming restored townhouses along gaslit streets.

This thirty-five-foot, six-ton bronze-and-copper statue of the Madonna overlooks East Boston from Orient Heights, about 216 feet above sea level. The Madonna Queen National Shrine was built with small contributions collected over more than fifty years by a Catholic missionary order of priests called the Don Orione Fathers, which also runs a nursing home in a former convent on the Heights. Dedicated in 1954, the statue is a replica of one atop Monte Mario in Rome sculpted by an Italian Jew, Arrigo Minerbi, as a gesture of gratitude to the order for helping him escape the Nazis during World War II. An observation deck in the tower offers unparalleled views of the airport below and the Financial District skyline just across the harbor. Comprised of five islands that were joined by landfill over 150 years, East Boston was one of America's first planned developments, its strict, gridlike pattern of streets a contrast to downtown Boston's crooked former cowpaths.

Above: *The conversion of a boarded-up storefront into the popular Bella Luna restaurant and arthouse by community activists in 1993 epitomizes the rebirth of Jamaica Plain from a comparatively neglected low-income neighborhood to a close-knit community of artists, young professionals, and South and Central American immigrants. Many of the grand old homes and business blocks have been redeveloped into juice bars, clubs, and coffeehouses. Bella Luna features live music, a weekly "psychic disco," variations of pizza named for local bands and singers, and a Sunday jazz brunch rated as the best in Boston. Jamaica Plain was named by the early Puritan settlers to honor Sir Francis Drake and his conquest of Jamaica.*

Right, top: *Competitors sign up at Doyle's Café for Doyle's Emerald Necklace Road Race, an annual five-mile run through Franklin Park. A Jamaica Plain landmark, Doyle's was opened in 1882 by the Doyle family and sold in 1971 to their friends, the amicable Burkes, who remain the proprietors. It serves up fifty different kinds of draft beer, one of the city's best clam chowders, and large helpings of ungarnished food—including corned beef and cabbage every Thursday. But Doyle's is best known as the stomping ground of pundits and politicians, from presidents to mayors; the walls are papered with political photographs and newspaper clippings.*

Right, center: *Established as an independent town in 1630, Boston's Dorchester section was a sparsely settled collection of villages and some mills clustered along the Neponset River. Still a sleepy backwater well into the nineteenth century, it began to grow with the arrival of the Old Colony Railroad, which made it a convenient place from which to commute into the city and which also spurred commercial development after the Civil War. Dorchester was annexed in 1870, but retains some small suburban-style neighborhoods of single-family homes like this Melville Avenue community.*

Right, bottom: *Saucer magnolias in Saint Leonard's Peace Garden in the North End. The first Italian church in New England, Saint Leonard's opened at Hanover and Prince Streets in the heart of the North End in 1873. Its Peace Garden is maintained by the Franciscan Friars as an oasis in the crowded neighborhood.*

"You need to learn tremendous skills to drive a car here, or even to navigate. That's why Boston has so many colleges and it's also why so many of the professors always look lost."
—**Marc Abrahams, editor,**
Annals of Improbable Research

Above: *Boston's large Asian population is scattered around the city and its suburbs, but newer immigrants with little English language knowledge tend to congregate in Chinatown and work in its restaurants, garment factories, and other businesses. Chinatown hosts many Asian cultural events, including the Lion Dance of the August Moon Festival, which is pictured here.*

Left: *A gift from Taiwan in 1982, this massive ceramic gate marks the traditional entrance to Boston's Chinatown section, which is bordered by Harrison, Kneeland, Hudson, and Beach Streets. Some Chinese first came to Boston in the eighteenth century during trade with the Far East, but larger scale immigration began in the 1870s. By 1900, there were about five hundred Chinese in Boston. Most of the neighborhood that would become Chinatown once marked the water's edge of the original peninsula, but the bay was filled during the 1830s for the new Boston & Worcester Railroad terminal and yards.*

Roxbury was one of the most affluent towns in colonial America, thanks to its location close to Boston, its rich pasture- and farmland, and its location on the Stony Brook, which offered excellent sites for early industry. Annexed in 1867, Roxbury began filling up with Irish, German, and Polish immigrants, who arrived aboard the spreading elevated railway and streetcar lines, since dismantled. Dudley Square remains the busy center of the community, which now is predominantly black. This mural of the "Faces of Dudley" was painted by the Boston Youth Cleanup Corps.

Designed by Frederick Law Olmsted to be a typical example of the New England woods, the wilderness preserve on the west side of Franklin Park was disturbed during landscaping of the park only enough to thin out the trees and build walkways and bridle paths that follow the curving contours of the land. Ninety-nine wide steps carved from Roxbury puddingstone lead to the one-hundred-acre forest. Diamond-shaped, one-mile-square Franklin Park was added to the National Register of Historic Places in 1971.

Above, left: *Boston's oldest neighborhood, the densely settled North End has been home to almost every immigrant group that passed through Boston. Today it is distinctively Italian, its narrow streets lined with restaurants, pastry shops, and trattorias. Many residents escape the crowds on roofdecks with unequaled views of the neighboring Financial District.*

Above, right: *Built in 1870 by Aaron Davis Williams Jr. out of Roxbury puddingstone and Nova Scotia sandstone, this neo-Gothic mansion in Roxbury called Oak Blend now houses the Museum of the National Center of Afro-American Artists, the only art museum in New England devoted exclusively to African, Carribean, and African American fine arts. Opened in 1969, the museum features joint exhibitions with the Museum of Fine Arts and other institutions and permanently displays a re-creation of the coffin, sarcophagus, and burial chamber of a Nubian king.*

"Three disparate aspects of Boston and Cambridge make it a remarkable place to live and work: the ever-changing quality of light and skyline as I jog beside the Charles River in the early morning, the unique and vibrant intellectual community of faculty and students within which I am privileged to work, and the ease with which one can get from place to place within the compact, history-laden city of Boston."
—Massachusetts Institute of Technology President Charles M. Vest

Above: *The South End, viewed from the observation deck at the top of the Prudential building. The entire neighborhood is a national historic district, the country's biggest. Long home to successions of immigrants, it has been gentrified by artists, writers, and others drawn by the red-brick rowhouses, tranquil streets, and trendy restaurants. The Boston Center for the Arts, the Boston Ballet, and Holy Cross Cathedral, seat of the Archdiocese of Boston, all call the South End home.*

Right: *An antique fair and flea market at the Cyclorama Building in the South End. Designed in 1884 to house a four-hundred-by-fifty-foot cyclorama of the Battle of Gettysburg that drew huge crowds, the Cyclorama later hosted boxing matches, many featuring legendary Boston prize-fighter John L. Sullivan, and served as the city's flower market until 1968. The building is listed on the National Register of Historic Places and is run by the Boston Center for the Arts.*

"Boston breeds the world's best bargain-hunters."
—Sam Gerson, chairman and chief executive officer,
Filene's Basement

The L Street Brownies take a February dip in Boston Harbor. Organized in 1902 under the philosophy that bracing, mid-winter swims prolong life, the L Street Brownies take the plunge year-round from the beach beside the L Street Bath House in South Boston—most notably on New Year's Day, when hundreds of hangers-on dive with them into the chilly water. There are nine public ocean beaches within the city limits.

Corned beef, cabbage, and good-natured insults are served in equal portions at the annual St. Patrick's Day breakfast in South Boston. Presided over by the neighborhood's sitting senior state legislator, the annual tradition was begun in 1957 by then–Senate Minority Leader John Powers. Politicians and business leaders of all backgrounds exchange barbs in front of a banner reading Cèad mìle fàilte, Irish for "100,000 Welcomes," in a union hall decked out in green, white, orange, red, and blue.

Two of the winners of the annual red hair competition; the prize is a ride in the South Boston St. Patrick's Day Parade. A tradition since 1901, the parade was sponsored by the city until 1947, when the South Boston Allied War Veterans took it over. In election years, it still attracts campaigning politicians of all creeds. The red hair contest was added in 1995.

Index

Where to Go for More Information

The Greater Boston Convention and Visitors Bureau. Prudential Tower, Suite 400, PO Box 990468, Boston, MA 02199. (888) SEE-BOSTON. **Information available:** Provides the official visitor information kit; dining and shopping guides, including discount coupons; and a publication for families called *Kids Love Boston*, complete with games to play in the car. Also offers Boston By Phone, a service that connects directly to area attractions, accommodations, and restaurants.

Massachusetts Office of Travel and Tourism. 100 Cambridge Street, 13th Floor, Boston, MA 02202. (800) 447-6277. **Information available:** Offers a free vacation planner covering all regions of the Commonwealth of Massachusetts.

About the Author
and Photographer

Photo © Furnald/Gray

Author Jon Marcus is a lifelong New Englander, born in Boston and schooled in Maine, who began his professional career on Cape Cod. He is a graduate of Bates College, Oxford University, and the Graduate School of Journalism at Columbia University.

Marcus has written about travel for *Yankee, Conde Nast Traveler, Travel Weekly,* and other magazines, as well as the *Boston Globe, Baltimore Sun, Chicago Tribune, Dallas Morning News, Detroit Free-Press, Houston Post, Los Angeles Times, Miami Herald, Newsday, St. Louis Post-Dispatch, St. Paul Pioneer-Press, Washington Post,* and other newspapers.

A senior editor for *Boston Magazine* and a U.S. education correspondent for the *Times* of London, he has won several journalism awards.

Photo © Gary M. Blazon

Photographer Susan Cole Kelly specializes in photographing the beauty of the American landscape with the intimate details of both places and people.

Kelly majored in art at the University of New Hampshire, studied photography at the New England School of Photography in Boston, and took masters classes at the Maine Photographic Workshop.

She is a contributor to the *Yankee Travel Guide to New England* and the *Alaskan Milepost,* and her photography has also appeared in *Vermont Life, Touring America, Down East,* and *Historic Traveler* magazines. Her images of Boston have been published in calendars and in postcard collections.

Kelly lives in Boston's North End.